Listening to Learning

To Barbara Taylor Bowman,
In honor of our beloved mentor and colleague,
Co-founder and past president of Erikson Institute,
Tireless advocate and leader in
Promoting high-quality education for young children.

Listening to Learning
Assessing and Teaching Young Children

Gillian Dowley McNamee

Jie-Qi Chen

For information:

Corwin
A Sage Company
2455 Teller Road
Thousand Oaks, California 91320
(800) 233-9936
www.corwin.com

Sage Publications Ltd.
1 Oliver's Yard
55 City Road
London EC1Y 1SP
United Kingdom

Sage Publications India Pvt. Ltd.
Unit No 323-333, Third Floor, F-Block
International Trade Tower Nehru Place
New Delhi 110 019
India

Sage Publications Asia-Pacific Pte. Ltd.
18 Cross Street #10-10/11/12
China Square Central
Singapore 048423

Vice President and Editorial Director:
  Monica Eckman
Publisher: Jessica Allan
Content Development Editor:
  Mia Rodriguez
Content Development Manager: Lucas
  Schleicher
Senior Editorial Assistant: Natalie Delpino
Production Editor: Vijayakumar
Copy Editor: Ritika Sharma
Typesetter: TNQ Tech Pvt. Ltd.
Proofreader: Girish Kumar Sharma
Indexer: TNQ Tech Pvt. Ltd.
Cover Designer: Candice Harman
Marketing Manager: Olivia Bartlett

Printed in the United States of America

Library of Congress Cataloging-in-Publication Data

Names: McNamee, Gillian Dowley, author. | Chen, Jie-Qi, author.

Title: Listening to learning : assessing and teaching young children / Gillian Dowley McNamee, Jie-Qi Chen.

Description: First edition. | Thousand Oaks, California : Corwin Press, [2024] | Includes bibliographical references and index.

Identifiers: LCCN 2024000890 | ISBN 9781071889213 (paperback : acid-free paper) | ISBN 9781071889244 (adobe pdf) | ISBN 9781071889220 (epub) | ISBN 9781071889237 (epub)

Subjects: LCSH: Early childhood education--United States. | Curriculum-based assessment--United States. | Curriculum planning--United States. | Performance in children.

Classification: LCC LB1139.25 .M466 2024 | DDC 372.210973--dc23/eng/20240129

LC record available at https://lccn.loc.gov/2024000890

This book is printed on acid-free paper.

24 25 26 27 28 10 9 8 7 6 5 4 3 2 1

Contents

· ·

Section II. *Bridging* Assessment Activities   57

Chapter 6: Pretend Play   59

Chapter 7: Dictating and Acting Out a Story   71

Chapter 8: Counting Collections   87

Chapter 9: Drawing a Self-Portrait   99

Chapter 10: Strong House for the Three Pigs   111

Visit the companion website at
https://resources.corwin.com/ListeningToLearning
for downloadable resources.

List of Tables and Figures

Tables

Figures

List of Companion Website Resources

 Full-page reproducible sheets of the following items can be found on the companion website at **https://resources.corwin.com/ListeningToLearning**

Activity Recording Sheets (Appendix A)

- Pretend Play Recording Sheet
- Dictating a Story Recording Sheet
- Acting Out a Story Recording Sheet
- Counting Collections Recording Sheet
- Self-Portrait Recording Sheet
- Strong House for the Three Pigs Recording Sheet

Performance Rubrics (Appendix B)

- Pretend Play Performance Rubric
- Dictating a Story Performance Rubric
- Acting Out a Story Performance Rubric
- Counting Collections Performance Rubric
- Self-Portrait Performance Rubric
- Strong House for the Three Pigs Performance Rubric

Working Approaches Rubrics (Appendix C)

- Productive Working Approach Rubric
- Descriptive Working Approach Rubric

A Child's Learning Profile Summary (Appendix D)

- A Child Learning's Profile Summary

About the Authors

Gillian Dowley McNamee, Ph.D., is a Professor emeritus of child development and early childhood teacher education at Erikson Institute, Chicago, Illinois. She has worked with early childhood teacher candidates during their preparation for public school teaching as well as long term with teachers working with children growing up in challenging social and economic situations. Gillian has carried out professional development initiatives with teachers across the United States, Europe, Taiwan, several regions of China, Turkey, and Kyrgyzstan. She speaks nationally and internationally on how teachers can listen to young children in order to become the teacher young children need to secure their future. Dr. McNamee's expertise is in language and literacy development, and in the work of Russian psychologist, L. Vygotsky as applied to early childhood settings. She has worked extensively with the story telling and story acting activities developed by Vivian Paley. She has been a Spencer Fellow with the National Academy of Education, and recipient of one of the first Sunny Days Award from Children's Television Workshop/Sesame Street Parents for her work developing an innovative early childhood teacher preparation program.

Jie-Qi Chen, Ph.D., holds the Barbara T. Bowman Professorship in Early Education at Erikson Institute. Beginning as a teacher in various classroom settings, from toddlers to middle school, she has devoted three decades to teacher professional development. Dr. Chen founded the Early Math Collaborative at Erikson, a groundbreaking initiative that revitalized early mathematics education and empowered teachers to emphasize foundational math concepts. Her career spans expertise in early math education, classroom assessment, the educational impact of multiple intelligence theory, and teacher development. With 17 authored and edited books, translated into multiple languages, her contributions are widely recognized. Dr. Chen's previous roles include Fulbright Senior Specialist in Education, consultant to the

United Nations Children's Fund, and membership in boards such as Scholastic Education's Early Childhood Advisory Board and the National Association for the Education of Young Children's Governing Board. Currently, she serves as a director at the National Board for Professional Teaching Standards.

Acknowledgments

· ·

We thank our colleagues, Ann Masur, Jennifer McCray, and Luisiana Melendez, whose years of work with us in the early 2000s contributed to the development of the *Bridging* framework and activities offered in this book.

Our gratitude also goes to our teacher educator colleagues Jeanine Brownell, Mary-Hynes Berry, Rebeca Itzkowich, Donna Johnson, and Liz Tertell for their feedback on the initial draft of this book. Their profound understanding of content knowledge and classroom practice significantly strengthens the connections between assessment and teaching.

We thank the many early childhood teachers and student teachers we have had the chance to work with over many decades. Each one of you helped us grow more sensitive to and more thoughtful about the challenges teachers face in every moment of the school day when the lives of a large group of growing children are under our supervision in our hands and hearts.

We are deeply grateful to our own mentoring teachers we benefitted from as we began our careers as classroom teachers and who continue to inspire us to understand the dynamics of what we think is the greatest honor: to be called Teacher.

Our immense appreciation also goes to the remarkable Sarah Roggio. Through her meticulous editing expertise, she contributed to enhancing the book's overall structure and language, ensuring its clarity, precision, and readability. We cannot thank her enough for her invaluable edits.

Finally, we thank Barbara Taylor Bowman, a co-founder of Erikson Institute in 1966, for her unwavering support of excellence in early childhood teaching. Her career of 60+ years has been advocating for skilled knowledgeable teachers who have a vision they can articulate for what they teach young children, why they teach, and how they do it. She has been our mentor, colleague, our boss, and our friend – the best kind. She never stops asking hard questions! We dedicate this book to her and the children that benefit from the excellence she insists on – the children in families of every race, language and dialect, cultural background, and economic class in our communities close to home and around the world.

Publisher's Acknowledgments

Corwin gratefully acknowledges the contributions of the following reviewers:

Catherine Cloran
Teacher
Los Alamos Public Schools
Los Alamos, New Mexico

Christine Ruder
Second-Grade Teacher
Rolla Public Schools
Rolla, Missouri

SECTION I
OVERVIEW

Introduction: Listening to Learning

CHAPTER
#1

- What is *Bridging*?
- How Does *Bridging* Differ From Other Child Assessments?
- Who Are the Primary Users of *Bridging*?
- How Does This Book Differ From the Previous Edition?
- How Is This Book Organized?

When we started teaching young children, we wanted to be proficient and skilled in our daily work with them. We participated in student teaching and watched more experienced teachers carry out lessons. In our early years of teaching, we often felt frustrated that we were not able to put into practice the many details in our minds. Too often, the details felt like a jumble of educational goals, images of effective practice, advice from colleagues about managing immediate situations with children, and what our own experiences suggested we try. We often had difficulty articulating what was not working and why. We were not always sure what would help close the gap between our less-skilled attempts to teach and the work of experienced teachers whose orchestrating of learning unfolds smoothly, efficiently, and in a well-organized way.

Effective teaching derives from a sense of agency — a sense of awareness and certainty that professionals bring to decisions that must be made nonstop throughout the day while "not missing a beat." An important fact about effective teaching skills is that they are learned — every single one of the skills involved. As educators, we can and need to be able to delineate, account for, and practice the skills involved. *Listening to Learning* sets out a pathway to effective teaching of children aged three to six while uncovering the skills and decisions that teachers make when they observe and listen carefully to their children.

The most basic teaching skills that all teachers and childcare providers learn are observing children and listening to what they say for clues about what they are learning – about letters and numbers, ideas and other people – how to make friends, how to discuss problems and come to new understandings. Our colleague, Sam Meisels, reminds us that the word *assessment* comes from the old Latin word meaning, "to sit alongside of," to listen without judging, and, instead, listen for understanding. That is the meaning that we bring to the processes of assessing and getting to know children that can strengthen teaching that we offer in this book. We describe how early childhood professionals can assess children while they are engaged in everyday learning activities by listening to their thinking in order to understand how to more effectively teach and guide their learning. The tool and process we introduce for this is called *Bridging*.

The *Bridging* assessment process offers a structure for novice teachers and childcare providers as well as veteran professionals to notice how they set up opportunities for children to learn in different curricular activities. Having prepared the environment with materials and set the schedule for the day, teachers and providers then observe and listen carefully for what children know and can do. Furthermore, they discover what learning is unfolding in this moment in time for each child along with noticing what factors might strengthen and enhance their learning such as adjusting the materials being used, the set-up of the activity, and how children work in various groupings. In this way, teachers learn how to strengthen and refine their teaching through learning to assess children. Thus, we offer a pathway to effective teaching grounded in teachers assessing children in everyday activities by sitting alongside them in order to get to know them better and become the teacher that the children need. The following vignette illustrates the *Bridging* process in action.

Once upon a time, a little girl, she ride on the pony. Then she flew with the eagles. And she went home and got dressed for school. Then she ride on a helicopter and ride on a ghost.

Ms. Drake approaches a table where several four-year-old boys are making puzzles. She asks if anyone has a story they'd like to tell today that she will write down for them. Two boys, Maurice and Gabriel, eagerly respond, "I do!" Maurice takes the lead and begins dictating his imaginative story, with Gabriel listening intently.

When he's done, Ms. Drake says, "Maurice, great story! I think the group will like the idea of the girl flying with the eagles. We will act this out at group time." Ms. Drake then asks Gabriel if he wants to tell a story, and he responds eagerly with, "Yes!" This time, it's Maurice's turn to listen.

In these few minutes of the school day, Ms. Drake has engaged these two boys in an assessment process using the tool *Bridging*. As the boys' teacher, Ms. Drake is an active participant in this assessment activity. She is not an outside testing specialist administering an assessment divorced from the events and context of the school day. On the contrary, Ms. Drake seamlessly integrates this *Bridging* assessment activity into the school day's natural flow of events. As she listens to these two children and writes down their stories, she has a prime opportunity to sample and assess her children's narrative skills, oral language expression, and creative spontaneity. In her classroom, the *Bridging* assessment process is fully integrated into the curriculum, becoming an essential and organic aspect of the learning environment.

What Is *Bridging*?

Bridging is a structured, observational assessment tool for children aged three to six who are in childcare settings, preschool, or kindergarten. The structure consists of five routine instructional activities commonly used in many early childhood settings. The five activities represent key content areas of learning for young children. These content areas build the foundations for thinking and problem-solving in learning to read and write; mathematics; the visual arts; and science, technology, engineering, and mathematics (STEM). The activities include pretend play, dictating and acting out children's stories, counting collections, drawing a self-portrait, and building strong houses for the three pigs. Table 1.1 provides a summary of the five *Bridging* activities.

An instructional routine is a structured and systematic approach that educators use to guide and organize the teaching and learning process in an early childhood setting. It is a consistent and repeatable sequence of activities designed to achieve specific educational objectives such as the daily practice of reading storybooks to young children. Instructional

Table 1.1 *Bridging* Curriculum Areas and Assessment Activities

CURRICULUM AREAS	ASSESSMENT ACTIVITIES
Cross-content Learning	**Pretend Play:** Children learn to engage in sustained imaginative role-playing activities to foster creativity and symbolic thinking as well as listening and social skills.
Language and Literacy	**Dictating and Acting out a Story:** Children tell a short impromptu story one-on-one with the teacher who writes it down, reads it back to the child to ensure clarity and accuracy, and finally, at a group time, invites the class to act out the stories they have created.
Mathematics	**Counting Collections:** Children count items to determine how many are in a "collection" of objects. Then they draw and/or make a written representation of how many they counted and how they counted.
Visual Arts	**Drawing a Self-Portrait:** Children use a pencil to create a self-portrait portraying themselves with family members or friends at home, in childcare, or in school.
STEM	**Strong Houses for the Three Pigs:** Children use play doh or clay, craft sticks, and other materials to build houses for the pigs in *The Three Little Pigs* fairy tale.

routines provide a framework for teachers and childcare providers to deliver content, engage children, and facilitate learning effectively. As seen in Table 1.1, although the five instructional routine activities vary by content area and specific goals, they share the following characteristics in the *Bridging* assessment process.

▶ **Equitable:** Each activity has a low floor and a high ceiling, ensuring that children of different ages and skill levels can actively participate and thereby provide evidence of their competency and understanding. These activities offer ample and equitable opportunities for every child to shine. They also enable teachers and childcare providers to discern the diverse knowledge and skills that individual children bring to the group.

▶ **Developmental:** These activities build on extensive research work and field practice, ensuring that the key concepts and skills relevant to children aged three to six are sufficiently represented. Each activity includes a performance rubric that delineates the developmental pathways for the activity's key concepts and skills to emerge in young children's learning over the preschool and kindergarten years.

▶ **Economical:** The activities require minimal materials and little preparation and implementation time from the provider or teacher. The basic supplies including paper, pencils, and counting manipulatives are easily accessible and affordable, making the assessment process practical and viable for teachers and providers in any environment. This makes it possible for educators to devote their energy to understanding and supporting each child's learning.

▶ **Interactive:** Each activity draws children into an engaging learning environment that has built-in opportunities for them to collaborate and help each other. Examples include children working together to enact stories and construct a sturdy house for the three little pigs. Such activities not only enhance individual children's engagement and participation but also create a sense of connection and friendship with peers. As a result, children are more inclined to become focused and participate in the activity, which brings out their optimal performance.

Most importantly, the five routine instructional activities are used here to seamlessly bridge classroom assessment with the teaching and learning process, which is why we named this tool ***Bridging***. As an assessment tool, the activities serve as a dipstick to tap children's learning and skill development in five content areas that are foundational in early childhood education. In addition, these versatile activities can be implemented anytime during the school year, supporting children's development of key concepts and skills while documenting their progress in these essential curriculum areas. The predictability and familiarity of these routines create comfort and security for teachers and providers with their children, enabling a more effective focus on understanding the concepts and skills being learned.

Bridging empowers teachers and providers to monitor children's learning in real time, observing how children engage in everyday yet challenging activities. This curriculum-embedded assessment doesn't separate children from routine activities with isolated test questions to see what they know and can do. Instead, it uses specific, regularly occurring activities to examine children's learning up close – as if under a microscope – to better understand what and how children learn.

As teachers and childcare providers observe, document, and analyze children's learning across different curricular areas, *Bridging* enhances their ability to recognize key features of thinking and learning. This knowledge makes teachers and providers more skilled educators by informing their planning and implementation of upcoming lessons. Specifically, *Bridging* helps teachers and childcare providers reach the following goals:

- **Understanding key concepts and skills:** *Bridging* activities help teachers and providers develop a solid understanding of key concepts and skills in different content areas of learning that children aged three to six are working on;

- **Assessing the content and process of children's learning:** *Bridging* activities give teachers and providers information on how to identify children's current developmental accomplishments within each content area while also recognizing the working approaches children use in their learning; and

- **Understanding how to use assessment results to inform teaching:** Each *Bridging* activity description provides guidance on how to utilize the knowledge gained during the assessment process to help teachers and childcare providers refine and enhance their teaching practices. This guidance ensures that teachers and providers meet the diverse learning needs of children from various cultural, racial, ethnic, linguistic, and developmental backgrounds.

How Does *Bridging* Differ From Other Child Assessments?

Bridging serves a distinct purpose in facilitating early childhood teaching and learning. It is an assessment process, but it is neither a comprehensive curriculum assessment nor a state accountability tool measuring how much a student learned due to instruction. It also is not a developmental screening instrument for tracking whether a child meets typical developmental milestones. This tool is not designed to evaluate curriculum, teaching methods, or the overall quality of early childhood programs. In addition, *Bridging* activities are not add-on tasks to the school day.

Instead, *Bridging* offers a valuable child assessment process that involves gathering, organizing, and interpreting observations of children while they are engaged in their daily interactive learning activities. Teachers and childcare providers can assess children's real-time learning progress utilizing carefully established rubrics, which identify children's current developmental achievements and anticipated growth in the coming weeks and months. The rich and authentic information collected through *Bridging* can be used in parent conferences, school reports, or as sources of evidence of learning for mandated accountability assessments within the center, school, or district.

Moreover, *Bridging* activities not only offer insights into children's cognitive functioning but also shed light on the social supports and connections from their home, school, and community environments that contribute to their learning. Each variable that teachers and childcare providers identify, including social and emotional, linguistic, community, and cultural factors, enriches their understanding of the child. As teachers and providers adapt *Bridging* activities to cater to specific groups of children, the assessment process reaffirms the power, relevance, and enduring impact of learning for all children in their diverse and unique contexts.

In early childhood classrooms, teachers prefer assessing children through ongoing observation in an authentic learning environment rather than relying on traditional "sit-down" paper-and-pencil approaches. *Bridging* is an example of such an authentic assessment. Although this form of assessment is generally preferred, it does come with challenges. One significant drawback is that it takes time and cannot be done quickly in a single sitting. Moreover, a risk exists that certain behaviors or skills may not naturally emerge or be adequately observed by teachers or providers, especially for children of a different culture or race than the teacher or provider, and for those with English as a second language. Some children may initially be reticent, or their behaviors may not be fully understood by teachers and providers (Curenton et al., 2020).

The *Bridging* approach offers a solution by using five routine learning activities as the centerpiece of the assessment. These five activities are manageable for classroom teachers and childcare providers while addressing essential curriculum content areas for early learning. They can be readily carried out while providing a structured framework for capturing children's awareness of and proficiency with important basic skills and concepts. Another key feature of *Bridging* is that all children participate in the same activities. This approach ensures equitable assessment of the instruction given, materials used, and procedures followed. These activities also are designed to connect readily with children's home and community experiences, enabling teachers and providers to learn about children's funds of knowledge through storytelling, drawing, pretend play, and counting games.

Bridging also stands apart from other observational assessments through its explicit and direct connection to classroom teaching and learning. The *Bridging* assessment process begins with teachers and childcare providers observing children engaging in various routine instructional activities across different curricular areas. These simple routines can be continuously implemented in the classroom to support children's growing proficiency with concepts and skills in the five curricular areas. Thus, *Bridging* fosters an ongoing process of observation and assessment, allowing for continuous refinement in teaching. By directly linking assessment to daily teaching and learning activities, *Bridging* narrows the gap between assessment and instructional practices.

Who Are the Primary Users of *Bridging*?

The primary users of *Bridging* are early childhood professionals involved in the care and education of young children three to six years of age. This includes preservice teacher educators and their student teachers and childcare professionals as well as in-service professional development providers supporting classroom teachers and providers working in early childhood classrooms and family or kin childcare settings.

For preservice teacher preparation programs, we have used the *Bridging* assessment process in several courses teacher education students take – including assessment courses, curriculum methods courses, and student teaching seminars. For example, when our students were required to complete the edTPA (a national teacher performance licensing assessment), the *Bridging* process equipped them to effectively plan, implement, and assess children's learning in small-group activities. The *Bridging* assessment activities are highly applicable to the edTPA assessment process because they are derived from the early childhood curriculum and offer valuable insights into carefully observing what children learn and how they approach challenges (Chen & McNamee, 2006; McNamee et al., 2008).

Professional development providers can also use *Bridging* to support teachers and childcare providers in several ways. First, this tool helps early childhood professionals hone their observational skills. Second, it deepens their understanding of key concepts and skills in essential early childhood curriculum areas. It also enables them to identify developmental progress markers between aged three and six. Finally, *Bridging* helps educators see that classroom assessment and effective teaching are two sides of the same coin. Early childhood educators can conduct professional learning sessions to engage teachers in understanding how to implement Bridging as *both* an instructional practice and an assessment tool in the classroom. This book provides the necessary materials for these professional development sessions, including the conceptual framework for the tool and process, activity descriptions, assessment rubrics, and suggestions for further teaching.

For childcare providers and those who support them whether it be in center-based or home-based settings, *Bridging* provides a lens into the common early childhood activities they are likely providing for young children such as pretend play, drawing activities, and opportunities to count. *Bridging* activities give providers and those they interact with a means to ensure that children are receiving quality care and education along with a way to talk about what children are learning and how they learn over time. *Bridging* activities can be carried out with two or three children, or with children participating in a classroom alongside 18–20 peers.

While individual teachers or providers can use *Bridging* in their classrooms or home care settings, its potential is even greater when teachers and providers collaborate on an ongoing basis. By providing a set of activities covering both preschool and kindergarten years, *Bridging* offers teachers and providers a shared lens and common language to discuss, compare, and reflect on their teaching experiences and children's learning. These professional discussions among teachers and providers play a crucial role in building and maintaining a cohesive program. Moreover, they enable teachers and providers to articulate and refine their approaches to meeting the diverse needs of all children during the crucial early childhood years when the foundation for school learning is being established.

Teachers and providers thrive when compatible working relationships exist with colleagues both within and across grade levels. *Bridging* can bring teachers and providers together to address shared goals by increasing their understanding of children's learning from one year to the next in integrated, sustained, and generative ways. For an early childhood program to be strong and effective, the teachers, providers, and administrators need a shared vision and curricular pathway to achieve desired outcomes. Educators' responsibilities are not complete until their individual effort joins with the talents of colleagues to contribute to meeting the mission and goals of the school. *Bridging* supports the development of such professional learning communities among teachers, providers, and school or childcare agency administrators.

How Does This Book Differ From the Previous Edition?

In 2007, we published *Bridging: Assessment for Teaching and Learning in Early Childhood Classrooms, PreK–3,* with Corwin Press after years of research and fieldwork. The *Bridging* assessment in the 2007 edition consists of 15 activities in five content areas: language arts and literacy, visual arts, mathematics, sciences, and performing arts. Over the last 15 years, our student teachers have used *Bridging* assessment activities in their classrooms with young children. We also have offered *Bridging* professional development to teachers nationally and internationally.

Teacher educators across the country have written to us about their experiences using *Bridging* assessment activities.

This new edition incorporates significant revisions resulting from our insights and feedback from colleagues who have used the tool with pre-service and in-service teachers. Additionally, we have considered the changes in the field of classroom assessment in early education. In this updated edition, we focus the assessment process on the preschool and kindergarten years, instead of spanning from preschool through third grade. This more targeted age range ensures that the assessment process, performance rubric, and suggestions for *Bridging* assessment to teaching are developmentally appropriate for this hardest of all age groups to assess. (Chapter 3 will go into more detail on the challenges involved.)

In this updated edition, we have streamlined the content, reducing the number of activities from 15 to 5. This makes it more manageable for teachers and childcare providers to incorporate the activities into their regular teaching practice. A departure from the last edition is the high-lighting of the role of instructional routines in the *Bridging* assessment process in this edition. All five activities, whether newly developed or significantly revised, are designed to maintain their effectiveness in linking assessment results to the daily teaching and learning process.

The assessment of pretend play in this updated edition warrants special mention. We recognize the well-documented importance of play in a child's physical, social, emotional, cognitive, language, and creative development. Young children spend considerable time engaging in pre-tend play, but many early childhood professionals may lack specific knowledge on how to support it so that children reach their full potential. The pretend play activity in the *Bridging* assessment addresses this gap by outlining pathways in development and delineating indicators contributing to pretend play development in the early years. This gives early childhood educators valuable insights and a roadmap to support children's quality play experiences in school and childcare settings.

Despite these differences, the name of the assessment remains the same – *Bridging*. The overall message of *Bridging* also remains unchanged: effective classroom assessment is integrated into the curric-ulum to support child development and learning. This revised *Bridging* edition is tailored to meet the needs of teachers and childcare providers by giving them a valuable tool to engage in meaningful assessment and effective instruction.

How Is This Book Organized?

This book consists of three sections: this overview (Chapters 1–5), *Bridging* assessment activities (Chapters 6–10), and appendices. Chapter 1 provides an introduction to the *Bridging* approach of listening and observing young children learning while they are engaged in activities. Chapter 2 delves into *Bridging*'s approach to evaluating the content and process of children's learning. It includes a detailed description of how these two learning dimensions are assessed using performance rubrics and working approach rubrics. Additionally, this chapter outlines how to construct a child's learning profile to summarize the assessment results across all five activities.

In Chapter 3, the spotlight shifts to activity theory and the pivotal concept of "basic activities." This concept marks a theoretical break-through in the realm of assessment and serves as a guiding framework for *Bridging* assessment.

Chapter 4 focuses on educator agency within the *Bridging* assess-ment process. *Bridging* empowers teachers and childcare providers with flexibility and creative space to effectively tailoring the tool to address the specific needs of their students and attain targeted educational objectives.

Finally, Chapter 5 provides a case study that illustrates *Bridging*'s practical application within a classroom setting. This example illustrates the interrelatedness between assessment and teaching, highlighting *Bridging*'s unique advantage in fostering teacher and provider reflective practice and collaboration while concurrently achieving the goals of early childhood education for children aged three to six.

In Section II, Chapters 6 to 10 provide in-depth descriptions of the five assessment activities: pretend play, dictating and acting out stories, counting collections, drawing a self-portrait, and building strong houses for the three pigs. Each activity chapter starts with a brief introduction, followed by comments on the significance of the activity and its key concepts and skills. We then offer a snapshot of the assessment activity being conducted in an early childhood classroom, along with details on the materials needed and implementation procedures. To support teachers and providers in their diverse classrooms, each chapter con-cludes with "*Bridging* Assessment to Teaching" which offers options to further facilitate children's learning based on each child's learning profile.

Section III consists of the appendices which provide forms needed to conduct the *Bridging* assessment. For each assessment activity, the appendices include (1) recording sheets for teachers and providers to document what children do and say while working on the assessment task. The sheets also have space to record what children create in their design or thinking process (see Appendix A); (2) a performance rubric for each activity with indicators for each developmental level in completing the task as the child gains more knowledge and skill in that content area over time (see Appendix B); and (3) rubrics for the two working approaches – productive and descriptive – summarizing how children approach the task. Working approaches are the same across all five activities (see Appendix C). Finally, (4) we provide a "Child's Learning Profile Summary" sheet which organizes and summarizes each child's assessment findings across the five activities (see Appendix D). We also have included a glossary of assessment terms used throughout the text, making it easier for readers to understand the concepts presented.

Throughout the book, we have integrated classroom snapshots of teachers and childcare providers working with children in the different assessment tasks based on our experiences working with early childhood educators. These snapshots offer both inspiration and a realistic sense of the challenges teachers and providers face as they engage in the rewarding journey of planning for, overseeing, and orchestrating children's learning each day.

Listening to Learning opens a window for teachers and childcare providers to see the workings of learning and teaching unfold in front of them each day. Teaching and assessment of children's learning begins with the teacher or provider observing children while they engage in activities in varied curricular areas. Teachers and providers' observations are guided by specific rubrics that detail the developmental trajectories of children's learning and understanding in different subject areas, as well as the way they approach the learning tasks. Teachers and providers then continue the *Bridging* process by planning and implementing a curriculum based on the newly acquired knowledge of children's status in the content areas assessed. The unique feature of *Bridging* is the direct connection it makes between assessment findings and next steps in planning for tomorrow's learning. In this way, *Bridging* spans the often-wide chasm between assessment and curriculum by providing a seamless process that intertwines assessment with curriculum. The next chapter sets out the structure of the *Bridging* assessment tool.

Bridging: Assessing the Content and Process of Learning

CHAPTER 2

- Performance Rubrics to Assess the Content of Learning
- Working Approach Rubrics to Assess the Process of Learning
- *Bridging* Learning Profiles to Inform Next Steps in Teaching

*B*ridging assessment activities focus on uncovering the developmental progress of young children in relation to key concepts and skills in a range of curricular areas over a period of three to four years. Each *Bridging* activity has three rubrics to guide teachers and childcare providers in recording and analyzing children's efforts at a moment in time. One rubric assesses the level of children's performance on understanding key concepts and skills in content areas. The other two rubrics focus on children's working approaches during the activity, including how they respond to challenges, use materials, and interact with peers. These rubrics give teachers and childcare providers a clear roadmap to evaluate both a child's current level of development and areas that are emerging. As teachers and childcare providers come through the process, they are opening the way to new possibilities in their planning and teaching with questions such as, "How can I use this information to understand this child better? How does the child's role in this activity compare to that in other *Bridging* activities? What is making the difference in this child and others becoming so involved in learning activities?"

Performance Rubrics to Assess the Content of Learning

The content of learning in the five *Bridging* assessment activities is measured by tracking evidence of its key concepts and skills during children's performance. These key concepts and skills align with national and state early learning standards for children aged three to six. The five activities are generative to future learning in that they embody basic skills and understandings that children can gradually become more aware of and apply to new situations and problems over time. Rather than trying to evaluate children's knowledge of isolated facts and skills, the *Bridging* process provides activities that have meaning and purpose for children while also holding the skills and knowledge we seek for them to master. *Bridging* activities allow educators to watch the skills and knowledge develop while children are in the learning process.

Appendix B includes six performance rubrics for the five *Bridging* assessment activities. Dictating and acting out stories constitute one activity, but they are assessed using two distinct performance rubrics. Each *Bridging* performance rubric has six levels. Research in children's development and each content area of literacy, math, STEM, the arts, and pretend play, guided the rubric formulation. For example, the rubric for the children's dictated stories derives from Arthur Applebee's research on narrative development. This rubric also draws from extensive work studying Vivian Paley's implementation of the activities in a wide range of school and childcare settings. It includes utilizing these activities in Boston Public Schools, Houston early childhood programs, and Chicago area schools as well. The face validity of the rubrics was further established through consultation with content area experts as well as classroom teachers and childcare providers.

The *Bridging* rubric detailing the developmental shifts in each of the five activities enables teachers to identify a child's knowledge of key concepts and use of skills for a specific activity at a given time on a particular day. Each developmental level has both a name and specific performance indicators to assist the teacher in scoring a child's work. Table 2.1 provides a sample performance rubric.

An important aspect of the *Bridging* assessment process is the concept of listening in order to understand children and their learning at a moment in time, not judging them one way or another. In the *Bridging* assessment process, all rubric levels are interesting and helpful to a teacher or provider in understanding a child and the process of learning in a particular area of content learning. For example, Level 0, no performance or no participation does *not* mean no development. It means what it is – no participation on this day in that moment. This becomes interesting "data" to think about alongside other information a teacher gathers on a child, providing an opportunity for questions. For example, is the nonparticipation a one-time occurrence? Is nonparticipation the child's usual response to this particular activity? Does a particular type of material affect the child's participation or the grouping situation for the activity? Does the child prefer other types of activities for self-expression and participation? Nonparticipation, like any other rubric score, then becomes an opportunity to consider what the information gathered can tell us about children and how they benefit from an activity. For example, a child can benefit enormously from watching others dramatize a story instead of acting in one.

Over time, when teachers are using the *Bridging* assessment process, they are gathering a profile of learning scores that reveal a child's

Table 2.1   Sample Performance Rubric for Dictating a Story

LEVEL	NAME	PERFORMANCE INDICATORS
0	No Participation	• Child declines to participate in activity.
1	First Stories	• Child tells a one-word story such as "Mommy." Or "Running." • Child says one or more words, but without connections among the words. Story can sound like a list of items or events; for example, "A flower, a pencil, a bunny." • Child may scribble on paper and give one-word label or name to each object. • Story is one sentence (e.g., "A mermaid swims in the water.")
2	Sequence of Events	• Story elements share a common core because of some visible similarity (for example, a certain action repeated over and over or an "events of the day" story). • Story is a collection of ideas/objects/associations linked by some concrete similarity. • There is no single idea or character or problem at the center of the story. • Story might contain little detail or be a string of associations.
3	Primitive Narratives	• There is a core idea or character at the center of the story. • Relations among characters and actions are not fully developed. • The links among the characters and actions are based on practical experience in the here-and-now. The links are concrete rather than conceptual. • Story events lead from one to another but links may shift (settings may blur, characters may come and go).

Table 2.1 (Continued)

LEVEL	NAME	PERFORMANCE INDICATORS
4	Unfocused Chain	• Story line is tenuous and often gives way to another topic • Story events lead from one to another but links may shift over the course of the story. • Links among story events are often based in the here-and-now and are concrete
5	Focused Chain – Problems and Plots Emerge	• Story is well developed in terms of events and actions of characters • The story plot proceeds with a central idea or conflict that is concrete rather than conceptual (for example, a baby is sick and needs to go to the doctor, or a princess has to find her lost sister, or good guys have to stop pirates from kidnapping the captain) • Stories can be a "continuous adventures of ___" type narrative
6	Elaborate Narrative	• Story unfolds with a set of events and characters around a central idea or problem with consistent forward movement toward problem resolution at a conceptual level (for example, a lonely fox has no friends and finds a lost rabbit. Will the fox scare it or find a way to make friends?) • Story has a climax where there is change in a character or circumstances as a result of events or characters' actions. • Story includes some description of characters motivations and indicators of change

Source: Adapted from Applebee (1978).

strengths and interests – as well as areas of development that are still unfolding and that can benefit from experiences, guidance, and coaching. Teachers and providers are also gathering a wealth of information about variables that draw each child into learning in any one content area and into the learning environment more broadly. An uneven learning profile across the five activities is what we can expect in the *Bridging* process. Contrast and discrepancies in a child's performance across different activities pave the way for teachers and childcare providers to discuss how children learn in varied content areas. The findings across activities give teachers and providers new ways to determine where a child is thriving or struggling and consider how to best set up and carry out an activity to invite children's optimal performance.

Working Approach Rubrics to Assess the Process of Learning

To complement the documentation of the content that children already know or are learning, *Bridging* also helps teachers collect information on the process by which children engage when working on tasks. We use the term "working approaches" to define this process of learning. This term describes how a child interacts with materials and responds to the demands of a task. Teachers and providers observe a wide range of working approaches children use when engaged in a learning activity. For example, some children work with a solitary focus on what they are doing and cannot be distracted by anything until they complete their effort. Other children want to talk to others as they get oriented to a task and benefit from comparing notes with peers as they work. Some children jump right into a task, whereas others are slower to warm up to a particular task. *Bridging* includes an efficient way to capture such salient details about individual children's working approaches that significantly influence the outcome of a child's work.

For these rubrics, "working" indicates that the construct refers to a child's observable behaviors while engaged in an activity rather than the child's internal mental states or processes. "Approach" affirms that all children are actively participating in their learning as they engage in or respond to a task, rather than passively "having" a style. A child's working approach for each specific task and its relevant content area (math vs. creative expression vs. literacy) illuminates the child's executive functioning and self-regulation skills. These are the child's skills at attending to and focusing on what is important and necessary to complete the task successfully. For *Bridging*, working approaches are not a set of stable traits in the child and are not the same across all tasks. Rather, working approaches are malleable and affected by teacher guidance and coaching.

The process of learning in *Bridging* is measured through two types of working approach variables: productive working approaches that hinder or enhance performance and descriptive working approaches that describe characteristics or personality differences in how children engage in learning. Appendix C includes the two working approach rubrics which are the same across all *Bridging* assessment activities. Teachers and providers usually make a copy of the rubrics as a reference while noting children's behaviors and scoring their working approaches.

Two criteria guided our selection of the working approach variables. First, we reviewed studies of motivation, disposition, temperament, gender, personality, self-regulation, perceptual preference, learning styles, and executive functioning. This review helped us identify variables expected to either promote or hinder a child's performance, such as focus and attention during a task and resourcefulness when confronting a problem or challenge.

The second criterion we used to identify the working approach variables was their potential to help teachers recognize ways children learn in school. These working approach variables remind us that learning in school is not something children come into this new setting knowing how to do. They learn to go to childcare or school and then learn how to learn there. Once teachers and providers can recognize patterns in working approaches, they can guide children in this aspect of learning. For example, teachers can discuss with children how to focus when coming to a challenge, and what kinds of questions to ask themselves or one another.

We also ensured that the working approaches we identified for *Bridging* are observable in classroom and childcare settings. They apply to all children, not just to a few with strong tendencies toward one or more approaches. Each variable is described in terms that are meaningful to teachers and childcare providers. We kept the number of approaches manageable in the recording process. *Bridging* assesses ten working approaches that are observable across all five assessment activities.

Table 2.2 lists six *Bridging* productive working approaches: initial engagement in an activity, focus and attention throughout a task, goal orientation, planfulness, resourcefulness, and cooperation. These six working approach behaviors are assessed using a rating scale from 1 to 5. Higher scores indicate that a child's approach is more adaptive and organized and thus more conducive to successful participation in the classroom learning activity. It is important to note that the difference among children on a variable is a matter of degree.

When implementing *Bridging* activities across a wide range of early childhood classrooms, we found a positive correlation between children's working approach scores and their performance scores (Chen et al., 2011; Chen & McNamee, 2011). On average, a child who earns higher working approach scores also is likely to earn higher content rubric scores. Some working approach variables seem to have a greater impact on children's performance than others. Specifically, goal orientation, planfulness, and focus were more closely related to rubric scores than the other three approaches. This finding is consistent with research reporting that goal orientation and planfulness are among the central components of executive functions in higher mental processes. When teachers and providers

Table 2.2 Definition of Productive Working Approach Variables

VARIABLE	DEFINITION
Initial engagement	The extent to which the child responds to the activity when first introduced – evidenced by words, body language, and gestures.
Focus and attention	The degree to which the child is on-task throughout the activity, as evidenced by their attentiveness and persistence in working.
Goal orientation	The degree to which the child works toward the activity goal as set by the teacher, as evidenced by the child's behavior and use of materials.
Planfulness	The extent to which the child uses strategies to complete the task, as evidenced in conversation, use of materials, and sequencing of steps in the activity.
Resourcefulness	The extent to which the child seeks help from others to solve problems when needed.
Cooperation	The extent to which the child works well with peers when working on the task as evidenced by taking turns, sharing materials, and problem-solving with others.

become aware of the importance of such behaviors for thinking and learning, they are in a much stronger position to help children develop approaches that pave the way to successful learning.

In contrast to the productive working approach variables, several other characteristics of young children can make a difference in how they participate in learning and assessment tasks. The final four working approach variables are called descriptive working approaches because they do just that: highlight distinctive features of children's personalities that are ever-present in classroom dynamics. Table 2.3 defines these four descriptive approaches.

Like productive approaches, descriptive approaches are measured on a 5-point scale. However, unlike the productive working approach variables, higher scores on the descriptive variables do not indicate more effective ways of problem-solving or task completion. Instead, they indicate only that a child shows a greater degree of those behaviors and a stronger use of that approach for a specific task.

Descriptive approaches do not appear to impede or enhance performance. Rather, they provide another perspective on how a child approaches a task. As an example, consider the pace of work. A child working slowly on a task may be either careful and thorough or indifferent and passive. Similarly, a child who gets work done quickly may be careless and impulsive or experienced and skillful. Through systematic observation and documentation, a teacher or provider can determine how speed affects a child's work and whether a child's pace fluctuates or remains constant on tasks in different curricular areas.

Table 2.3   Definition of Descriptive Working Approach Variables

VARIABLE	DEFINITION
Chattiness	The amount of talking about matters connected to or possibly not directly related to the activity at hand such as personal concerns, fantasies the child engages in, or events outside of childcare or school.
Pace of work	The tempo or rhythm of a child's work in comparison to others in the group – faster, slower, or a more deliberate pace.
Social referencing	The extent to which the child is aware of others and checks in verbally or nonverbally during the activity when stuck or confused.
Playfulness	The degree to which the child shows a sense of humor during the activity, and/or a propensity toward imaginative pretend thinking with others while working.

Descriptive approaches may indirectly affect a child's performance by influencing the teacher's or provider's perception of the child. Children who score very high or very low on these approaches exhibit behaviors that may appear problematic for the child's learning from the teacher's or provider's point of view. For example, a very chatty child may seem inattentive and disruptive. A quiet child may appear disengaged and withdrawn. A serious child may seem to lack enthusiasm and interest. To the extent that teachers and providers see these as approaches rather than problematic traits, they gain an opportunity to consider what these behaviors mean from the child's point of view. With data from the *Bridging* assessment process, teachers and providers can look at when, how, and why a child uses these approaches. They also may find activities for which the child's use of these approaches is adaptive and helpful for others.

Take the example of a child who scores high on chattiness during a task. Through observation, the teacher or provider may learn that the child is very chatty only during tasks she works on independently. Being chatty appears to help the child relax and focus. Thus, what initially appeared to be disruptive behavior may be a strategy the child uses to achieve learning goals. If the teacher or provider curbs the child's chattiness, the child may find it more difficult to concentrate. By observing children's descriptive approaches, a teacher or provider gathers information about how to design learning environments that accommodate approaches that are beneficial for different children.

In the field of child assessment, what children learn and how they learn are rarely examined together. However, understanding a child's working approach can provide important insights when interpreting a child's performance level. Teachers and childcare providers recognize that children differ not only in performance levels or what they learn but also in how they acquire knowledge and skills. Working approaches help pinpoint the variables in the environments surrounding children that hinder or enhance their learning. These factors shape whether a child works in a setting that invites strengths or exacerbates vulnerabilities. Assessment of the working approach is sensitive to the influence of a child's motivation, executive functioning, emotional regulation skills, and the way social factors impact a child's work.

Bridging Learning Profiles to Inform Next Steps in Teaching

Bridging assessment results produce a learning profile, rather than a single score, to describe the child's learning progress at a moment in time. This profile specifies children's performance on all *Bridging* activities plus their two types of working approaches. Table 2.4 summarizes the information that a teacher collects for each child during a full round of assessment on the five activities. The learning profile form is provided in Appendix D.

Table 2.4 A Child's Learning Profile

Child's Name: Age: Gender: Observational Date:		Pretend Play **Cross-Content Learnings**	Dictating a Story **Language and Literacy**	Acting Out a Story **Language and Literacy**	Counting Collections **Math**	Self-Portrait **Visual Arts**	Strong House for the 3 Pigs **STEM**
Date of assessment							
Performance rubric score							
Productive Working Approaches	Initial engagement						
	Focus and attention						
	Planfulness						
	Goal orientation						
	Resourcefulness						
	Cooperation						
Descriptive Working Approaches	Chattiness						
	Pace of work						
	Social referencing						
	Playfulness						

By studying and discussing the unique patterns in each child's profile, teachers can make informed adjustments for individual children. At the same time, by noting the patterns of learning for groups of children during different activities, teachers and providers also gain insights into how to organize the flow of learning activities to support all children. Differentiating for individual children while also holding the learning of all children in mind and ensuring everyone's progress is an important skill teachers continue to cultivate in their practice.

From our research, we can illustrate how teachers have used *Bridging* learning profile data to understand individual children as well as the whole class. Figure 2.1 presents the profile for three kindergarten children's performance across *Bridging* activities. The observed variability – both within a child's rubric scores and across children's profiles – is striking. The profiles reflect exactly what teachers report: Children begin school with different experiences and exposure to activities that contribute to school-entry proficiency.

With a baseline profile of individuals and the entire class, the teacher can watch movement over time for both individuals and the group. The profiles make it clear that an average score or a limited sampling of curriculum areas can obscure the actual range of children's talents and performance levels on different sets of skills in the different content areas. At any one moment, children are working on different kinds of skills at different levels of competence in different curriculum content areas.

Another example of how constructing children's profiles can contribute to teacher insights is presented in Figure 2.2. In this graph, we see the assessment results for one child based on *Bridging* assessment data collected three times during a year: in October, February, and May.

Figure 2.1 *Bridging* Learning Profiles of Three Kindergarten Children

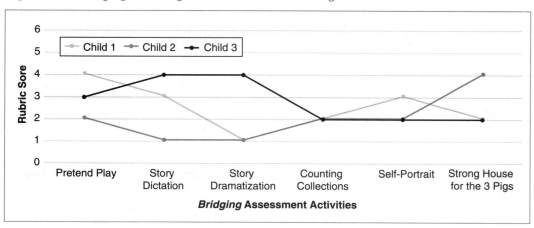

Figure 2.2 *Bridging* Learning Profiles of One Kindergarten Child Three Times a Year

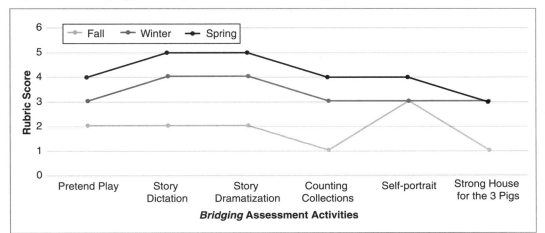

At all points, the child's profile is jagged – indicating that the child has enduring strengths and areas where the child is not as proficient. However, the patterns of unevenness shifted. In May, some areas were stronger than in October, whereas others had not kept pace. This profile reveals that performance at one point in time does not necessarily accurately predict a child's future developmental pathway.

Childcare and school learning experiences can advance a child's performance levels. For this to happen, however, an educator needs a framework to observe and understand the intersection between the path of each child's development and the course of development in that curriculum content domain. With the child and the learning domain in mind, the teacher and childcare provider then draws on various methods and makes decisions to stage both group and individual learning.

The purpose of constructing learning profiles is both to help teachers and providers understand each child as completely as possible and to give the educators the specific information they need to help every child meet educational goals. Using profiles makes it impossible to reduce the differences among children to simplistic rank ordering, with one child ranked higher than another. Rather, profiles reveal the complex nature of each child as a learner in terms of that child's interests, strengths, predispositions, and vulnerabilities. *Bridging* offers teachers more nuanced and specific information that points them to exactly what needs their attention. Chapter 3 explores the conceptual framework for *Bridging* that grounds this unique assessment for teaching and learning.

Basic Activities as the Unit of Analysis in *Bridging* Assessment

CHAPTER #3

- Unit of Analysis in Assessing Children's Learning

- *Bridging* Conceptual Framework: Basic Activities

- Child Development Grounding for *Bridging* Assessment Activities

In the *Bridging* assessment process, thinking and learning become visible as a child interacts with peers and the materials while engaged in a task. Utilizing the insights from L.S. Vygotsky along with A. Leont'ev's *Activity Theory* (1978), *Bridging* offers a shift in perspective that places the child performing an activity at the core of the assessment process. Since individual children do not think and learn in a vacuum, how can they accurately be assessed in one? In the *Bridging* process, assessment results derive from studying the details of the interaction among the child, teacher, or childcare provider, and the task at hand. To exclude any of these influences from the assessment process is to miss opportunities for understanding the child's learning in an educational setting in its full cultural context. Through *Bridging*, assessment and teaching become reciprocal processes because teaching is updated with each new insight teachers and childcare providers gain while observing and listening to children working in front of them.

This approach to assessing children stands in contrast to existing practices in educational and psychological research. Usually, a child is viewed as a discrete individual whose knowledge and skills can be evaluated and identified at a moment in time regardless of the circumstances surrounding the child. What the child can do or not do as well as what the child knows or does not know are seen as attributes of the child separate from any particulars of the task and context.

In contrast, when we center our analysis on the child participating in an activity, we gain insight into the intricate contextual factors that contribute to developmental changes over time. The context in school or a childcare setting is specified by the goals and purpose of a task that one or more children perform. The adults responsible for making decisions about what activities children participate in, when the activity takes place, what materials get used, and who works together become central in explaining findings and next steps in teaching. Changes that can be observed over time are analyzed and explained as a result of the dynamics among the child's efforts, the task parameters, and the instructions, guidance, and facilitation by the teacher or childcare provider. All three sources of influence are coordinated in explaining what happens in the child's effort on a task.

Unit of Analysis in Assessing Children's Learning

The practice of assessing children's learning and development traces back to Alfred Binet's pioneering work in developing the first known IQ test in 1904. While child assessment has evolved significantly over the years, one aspect has remained constant: the individual child continues to be the primary focus or unit of analysis in the assessment process. Various assessments – such as screening, diagnostic, readiness, and achievement tests – all aim to measure some dimension of a child. These dimensions include what the child can or cannot do, the child's strengths or weaknesses, and the child's mastery of skills. The individual child as a discrete autonomous being is the primary focus of – or the basic unit of – analysis in these assessment processes.

At times when the assessment context is considered along with the child's home life and previous experiences, these variables usually take a backseat when interpreting assessment results. Contextual information, such as the setting (e.g., home, childcare center, school, and community); the presence of others in the setting (e.g., peers, parents, teacher, or provider); and the child's familiarity with the specific task, are often regarded as "noise," controlled for, or even ignored. The primary goal of this type of assessment is to measure a child's behavior or performance while standardizing or putting in the background external factors. After assessment results are noted, professionals are often quick to make judgments about the child's home or community to explain what is lacking or underdeveloped in the child.

This approach has several shortcomings. When assessment focuses primarily on the child's performance as if it were occurring in a vacuum, it ignores the fact that children are fundamentally social beings – and their learning is socially negotiated or mediated every step of the way. Children learn through interactions with peers, parents, childcare providers, or teachers, as well as books, manipulatives, and digital media – and the nature of these interactions can hinder or promote learning. Moreover, as children learn and develop, they make sense of the world by interpreting societal and cultural expectations. They do this while using materials such as books, mathematical manipulatives, art materials, and technology as they actively participate with peers in informal and formal learning experiences.

Despite increasing recognition of the central importance of contextual factors in child development – including linguistic diversity, learning differences, cultural heritage, racial identity, and community experiences – these human factors still largely fall outside the parameters of an assessment process. This creates a serious problem; it leads us back into evaluating children by a set of criteria and expectations that often ascribes deficits to children who do not match the "expected norm," which is usually defined by white middle-class performance outcomes.

When children are seen as the sole, and even primary source and the cause of their own performance, their difficulties also will be seen as their own individual shortcomings. If, as a group, children do not meet performance goals, their racial and cultural group could be seen as the source of deficits. Performance is not understood to be the product of interactions between individual children and factors in the learning environment. Locating problems within the child only, we may hear educators describe some children as "slow learners" or as someone who "can't concentrate." Seeing learning difficulties only in terms of the child prevents teachers from closely examining factors such as the type of materials being used or the social dynamics of a small group that can influence children's learning and performance. Teachers can adjust and change such details to meet children's needs and enhance their learning *if* they are named and studied in the assessment process.

The *Bridging* assessment process differs from traditional assessments in a significant way in this regard. It focuses on recognizing, naming, and understanding the variations in how children respond to different activities. This approach is crucial for creating a fair, supportive, and responsive assessment process for all children, regardless of their race, ethnicity, culture, home language, or ability. The key to supporting each child's learning lies within these variations.

When teachers notice that adjusting materials or changing peer dynamics can impact a child's performance, that information becomes powerful because it can guide teachers in modifying various contextual factors to make learning more accessible for all children. For instance, they can invite children to help create an inventory of different classroom materials they want to count in the Counting Collections activity to increase their motivation and engagement. Teachers also can arrange small groups to work together on counting tasks, encouraging discussion and comparison of their counting strategies. When the assessment analysis process overlooks or sidesteps these contextual factors, teachers lose valuable information that could directly support children's learning. Ignoring contextual factors means neglecting half of the story about learning and teaching. The contextual factors are precisely the ones that teachers want to be aware of and utilize to promote the development of children's knowledge and skills.

Bridging Conceptual Framework: Basic Activities

Figure 3.1 provides a graphic representation of *Bridging*'s conceptual framework. In *Bridging* assessment activities, the child's performance is analyzed in context with the constraints and possibilities inherent to the activity, the materials utilized, and the child's interactions with peers and adults during the task. This assessment approach makes it possible to consider and discuss the multiple factors shaping a child's performance such as activity characteristics, teacher or provider influence, and the resources the child employs while participating in the specific task. By examining these interactions closely, we gain valuable insights into what the child knows and can do.

Task. Each *Bridging* assessment task represents an activity that encompasses essential content knowledge and skills aligned with national, state, and professional associations' learning standards for preschool and kindergarten children. Each of the five assessment tasks delineates the learning goals, key concepts, and skills that the task embodies in each curriculum content area. Each task also provides a list of materials necessary for children to carry out the activities. All tasks are designed to be open-ended in that they allow children to experiment with materials and interact with one another while teachers and childcare providers set appropriate boundaries.

By deliberately assessing across a range of content areas, *Bridging* provides opportunities for young children to exhibit their initial and early experiences with the concepts and skills in each discipline. By capturing

Figure 3.1 Conceptual Framework for *Bridging* Assessment

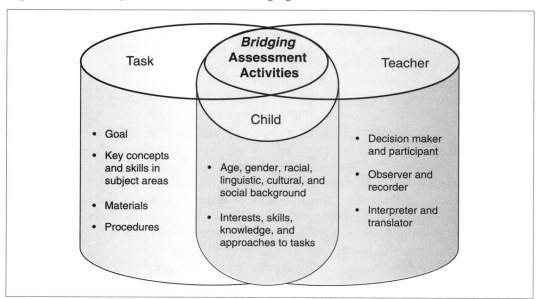

individual differences across various curriculum areas, *Bridging* illuminates the diverse developmental patterns present among children in every classroom. Recognizing and appreciating this diversity of intellectual talent and potential of young children helps teachers and childcare providers effectively support their learning and development by considering their strengths, interests, and approaches to learning.

The *Bridging* tasks align with the fundamental principles of the National Association for the Education of Young Children (2022), our profession's leading advocacy organization. Early childhood is a crucial period for recognizing and nurturing diverse talents because the full expression and development of children's abilities often occur later in adolescence or young adulthood. It is essential for educators of young children to acknowledge that each child in their class has the potential to make significant contributions to various fields such as medicine, literature, law, politics, business, science, and the arts. While the future holds many unknowns, exposing children to a variety of potential areas of expertise in the early years and building their proficiency in skills and knowledge across the curricular domains is critical. *Bridging* equips early childhood educators to assess and nurture the full range of human potential in their students.

Child. *Bridging* assessment emphasizes the need to systematically examine how children learn by observing their actions and interactions within peer groups, the provider's or teacher's decisions, and the assessment activity's context for that specific day. Children approach an assessment task with their unique age, racial, cultural, linguistic, and social background. By considering the child in the context of subject matter, materials used, and the teacher or provider's decisions, *Bridging* creates a dynamic assessment portrait that goes beyond a static assessment "result."

Focusing on the child in the context of a *Bridging* assessment activity does not disregard the child's unique interests, skills, knowledge, and personal approaches to tasks. On the contrary, the assessment data illuminate the child's distinctiveness in relation to various activity parameters. The primary focus of *Bridging* assessment is not solely the performance outcome but rather the outcome as it emerges from the child's interaction with peers and the teacher or provider while performing the task. *Bridging*'s focus is prospective, aiming toward the future rather than dwelling on the past. It informs teaching, learning, and development in the upcoming days and months, building on the child's observable achievements up to the present.

Teacher. In many assessment instruments used in schools today, early childhood educators are passive facilitators in the process. They administer a test protocol and receive results from a central administrative office that they are expected to use in curriculum planning. But teachers and childcare providers usually see no clear path from assessment results to classroom learning activities because the assessment is often imposed on the existing curriculum rather than integrated into it.

In addition, results often are delivered at a time removed from the time of the assessment. Teachers and providers usually conduct classroom assessments in a one-on-one situation that takes them away from instructional time as well. On the other hand, if the protocol asks teachers or providers to observe for skills and emerging knowledge in a natural classroom situation, this request often leaves teachers wondering what to observe and document.

This is not the case with *Bridging*. As Chapter 4 will discuss, teachers and childcare providers play a central role in gathering and interpreting data daily. They observe, reflect, make decisions, and actively participate at all points in the process. As active participants responsible for teaching and learning, teachers and childcare providers in the *Bridging* assessment process mediate the child's experience in learning activities. They also create circumstances that invite children to bring their knowledge and best effort to each task. In this process, the teacher and provider are sensitive to the child's abilities, skills, and strategies when approaching a challenge. Teachers and providers also observe the child's performance in relation to task components that they can adjust or change as needed. For instance, in the Counting Collections activity, teachers or providers may choose to group three or four children with similar mathematical abilities or varied skills, considering the appropriate challenge of collections for each individual child. Examining the decisions and choices by teachers and providers made during every phase of implementation reveals how they contribute to shaping the assessment process and the teaching process as well. This analysis effectively builds bridges that connect assessment findings with knowledge about how to fine-tune teaching. Through *Bridging*, teachers and providers can design experiences that create optimal support for children's learning – both individually and in a group.

Peg Griffin and Michael Cole elaborated on Leont'ev's activity theory to offer the concept of "basic activities" – a more in-depth way to explain how young children master basic skills. A basic activity speaks to the educational dilemma: How do educators promote the development of basic skills necessary for literacy and numeracy while achieving the goal of learning and teaching for meaning and understanding? Griffin and Cole proposed the concept of basic activities to integrate these seemingly disparate goals for learning. Table 3.1 below summarizes how *Bridging* activities meet the criteria for a basic activity.

Bridging activities are placed at the core of the assessment process to emphasize the significance of developmentally appropriate learning and intentional, social, challenging, meaningful, and engaging teaching methods. By making use of basic activities, *Bridging* establishes a connection between assessment and curriculum. It offers a lens to analyze a child's current development and promote future learning and growth while respecting each child's unique preferences and experiences. The *Bridging* assessment process encompasses a careful observation structure examining the interactions of the child and teacher or provider in the

Table 3.1 *Bridging* Activities Are Basic Activities

FOCUS	A BASIC ACTIVITY	*BRIDGING* ASSESSMENT ACTIVITY
Purpose and Goal:	• It has a purpose and meaning that children understand.	• *Bridging* presents a task with a clear goal that is developmentally appropriate for children aged 3–6.
Learning Process and Materials	• It capitalizes on the dynamic and social nature of children's learning processes and their interest in play.	• *Bridging* involves rich and engaging materials for children to use in playful situations, while also offering the necessary social support for children to showcase their best efforts and demonstrate their full capabilities.
Inclusivity and Peer Interaction	• It allows children at different skill levels and understanding to participate alongside one another.	• Each *Bridging* activity provides opportunities for children to work independently or collaboratively within the same age group and across different age levels, promoting ample peer exchange and collaboration.
Concept and Skill Development	• It introduces children to the basic skills necessary for completing and mastering the task.	• *Bridging* assessment recognizes the key concepts and skills identified in national standards embodied in each activity. Children get exposure to and practice with basic skills in the context of meaningful activities.
Assistance and Mastery	• It invites children's participation long before they can carry it out independently, while also enabling them to receive assistance from others during the initial stages of completion.	• It uses a six-level performance rubric to highlight the way children's understanding of key concepts and skills emerge and unfold over time with practice and interaction with others.
Emphasis on the Process of Learning	• It focuses not only on concepts and skills children are learning but also on how they acquire them, by respecting and accommodating their initial need for help with decision-making and selecting strategies to accomplish their steps.	• *Bridging* assessment process includes observations of children's working approaches, such as understanding the task's goal to its completion and awareness of and willingness to get help from others.

task at hand. The six developmental levels described in the performance rubrics for each *Bridging* activity make it clear that mastery of key concepts and skills requires time, involvement, effort, instruction, practice, and different forms of help over a period of years.

Child Development Grounding for *Bridging* Assessment Activities

Educators readily acknowledge that assessing children under the age of six is complex and can be unreliable. From age 3 to 6, children undergo enormous developmental changes. One significant change for most children during the early childhood years is joining a group of peers outside the home where they acquire new ideas alongside learning how to make friends and get along with others. In childcare and school, young children learn with and from each other. Children's understanding of people, ideas, and how the world works transforms in powerful and dramatic ways. Children have many ups and downs during these years: times of understanding and surging forward as well as times of getting confused and seemingly losing ground in their learning. Teachers and providers face many such paradoxes when trying to assess young children.

Development is content-specific and yet wholistic. Children's development is uneven across social, intellectual, physical, and emotional domains as well as across content areas such as literacy, numeracy, arts, and movement. Each content area in school learning proceeds on its own developmental pathway. At any point in time, a child may excel in learning in some areas (e.g., mathematics and drawing) but less so in others (e.g., in language-based activities such as storytelling or science, technology, engineering, and mathematics [STEM]). As a result, all children possess a jagged rather than an even learning profile across different content areas (as illustrated in Figures 2.1 and 2.2). These profiles also can change over several weeks or months.

Alongside content-area learning represented in the five *Bridging* activities, children are simultaneously learning how to handle new emotional challenges and social situations as well as becoming more physically agile. By assessing performance in a range of curricular areas for both what the child can do as well as tracking social and emotional indicators for how each child engages in these activities, *Bridging* captures individual differences in development that reflect the diversity of learners in every classroom. The breadth of its coverage enables teachers and childcare providers to see children from multiple perspectives rather than through a narrow academic window only. *Bridging* recognizes and values the diversity of children's intellectual talents and potential as well as relevant social and emotional variables developing simultaneously.

Development takes time and is nonlinear. Young children do not learn something once and then move on to mastering a new piece of knowledge or process of thinking. Their understanding of alphabet letters, number concepts, different kinds of narratives, and scientific inquiries can take months and even years to take root and mature into concepts and skills that children feel comfortable manipulating and discussing. Each day or week, they see and hear a new idea and learn a bit, but the idea is still under construction. From time to time, they may lose an understanding that we might have thought was already secure. Children need time to rework their understandings and connect new possibilities with those they have already considered. Instead of using different assessment activities for different age groups, *Bridging* applies the same ones across the four-year age span to allow children ample opportunities to revisit the key concepts and skills with increased understanding and mastery. Children with initial and sometimes shallow knowledge of the concepts develop a more solid understanding of the same concepts over time.

For this reason, it is helpful to have one rubric delineating milestones in the development of key concepts in each content area for age 3 to 6. When a child's story or drawing reflects a particular rubric level, teachers have a data point to guide their tracking of each child's progress. The child's next story or drawing may regress to an earlier rubric level when that child focuses on a new skill – such as how to tell a story that includes characters enacting a dialogue during a fight scene. Because a child is at one rubric level does not mean that he or she will be at the next rubric level in a few weeks and a subsequent higher rubric level a few weeks later. Children take steps forward and then back as they spend time working through understandings at different levels with different people in different circumstances. The *Bridging* assessment process helps teachers track this back-and-forth path in learning without passing judgment on these nonlinear steps but rather making room for this movement. *Bridging* helps teachers look more deeply for insight into what the child is focused on at any one moment and decide what support will help the child's effort.

Development is individualized. Young children come into childcare, preschool, and kindergarten classrooms with vastly different home-life experiences. Their learning often does not fit neatly and conveniently into academic school calendars. Early childhood teachers and childcare providers work to get to know each child and build a classroom community in which the enormous variability among children can support their play and work together as they build common ground for learning. *Bridging* activities are open-ended and allow children to engage regardless of their current level of skill and knowledge. For example, children tell their own stories and act them out, whether their story is one word, one sentence, or two paragraphs long. This variety of stories is part of everyday life in childcare settings, preschool, and kindergarten classrooms. From the children's point of view, all these stories invite possibilities.

Instead of focusing on standardized performance and expected outcomes for a grade level, *Bridging* emphasizes the individuality and variability that come with early childhood. Performance in *Bridging* activities is not built on expectations based on the child's age or grade level. Rather, they invite children to show where they fall on the full developmental trajectory of understanding the key concepts and skills in each of the five curricular assessment domains. Thus, *Bridging* activities illuminate where the child is and where they are headed in the coming days, weeks, months, and even years of schooling.

Development is social and contextualized. *Bridging* activities are carried out with groups of children in which a teacher or provider records an individual child's behavior when the child interacts with materials and peers. In addition to assessing children's understanding of key concepts and skills embodied in an activity, *Bridging* also looks at children's working approaches – the way they interact with materials and peers. Their learning in a content area is intertwined with each child's social, emotional, and cultural learning as well as physical development.

Young children benefit from working in groups because this supports them learning from and with others. Group work promotes social and emotional development as children learn to listen to and negotiate with others, take turns, and find ways to cooperate and collaborate with others. *Bridging* activities encourage children to express their ideas and understanding in words, which promotes their language and communication skills. Finally, working in groups invites children to learn from different perspectives on how to solve problems, which can broaden their understanding and deepen their learning. Learning in childcare and school is a social process for children, providers, and teachers alike.

Educator Agency in *Bridging* Assessment

CHAPTER
#4

- Classroom Snapshot: Ms. Curtis and Her Preschoolers

- Decision-Maker

- Participant

- Observer

- Interpreter

- Translator

Bridging affords us the chance to see the details teachers and child-care providers are considering in their decision-making before, during, and after a day with young children. *Bridging* offers guidance and support for the development of early childhood teachers' skills and knowledge while they are in the process of guiding their children's learning. By examining the work of skilled teaching in each activity, *Bridging* can help novice teachers and childcare providers find a path for moving toward the proficiency they seek. *Bridging* also helps more experienced early childhood professionals fine-tune, reflect on, and articulate what they are doing when things are going well for children in an activity as well as the skills they hope to further develop. In short, teachers and providers are in control of the *Bridging* process. This chapter helps teachers and providers become more aware of the decisions they are making through the school day that affect children's learning. Through the lens of the *Bridging* process, teachers and providers can examine their skills in teaching and monitoring young children's learning throughout the day and the school year and recognize the opportunities they are seeking to influence their children's learning.

Table 4.1 summarizes the thinking that teachers and childcare providers engage in while planning and carrying out *Bridging* assessment activities. The chart highlights the active decision-making role teachers and providers engage in during lessons and activities with their children all day long.

To provide a practical illustration of these *Bridging* roles, we offer a snapshot from a preschool classroom featuring Ms. Curtis and her

Table 4.1 Teacher and Childcare Provider Agency in the *Bridging* Assessment Process

ASSESSMENT PROCESS	EDUCATOR'S AGENCY
Before the assessment	• Consider ways to introduce the *Bridging* assessment activity to children. • Understand the key concepts and skills in the activity and the pathway of children's development in that content area. • Organize specific materials needed for the assessment activity. • Decide on the time of day to implement the assessment activity. • Invite children to participate in the activity and support their work throughout the process.
During the assessment	• Engage children in the assessment activity. • Observe children's behavior, gestures, and comments throughout the activity. • Record children's performance and working approaches on assessment activities using rubrics. • Take notes on each child's interactions with materials and peers.
After the assessment	• Look for patterns and relationships in a child's assessment performances and patterns for groups of children. • Seek to find strengths and areas needing further experience and attention in the near future. • Identify points of entry for individual children who need help in particular areas of the curriculum. • Use results to inform setting curriculum goals, selecting materials, and designing future learning activities.

four-year-old children. It highlights the work of a teacher in action. The discussion that follows provides an analysis of how effective teaching derives from the agency educators have in shaping the way a satisfying learning experience unfolds in a school day.

Classroom Snapshot: Ms. Curtis and Her Preschoolers

Ms. Curtis teaches preschool in a community-based center. It is early December in the school year. The recent Thanksgiving holiday and the approaching winter holiday break bring a flurry of intense activity to the children's play. Today the children's pretend play is grounded in the most important holiday to a young child: having a birthday. The following notes reflect our edited version of Ms. Curtis's account of what happened that morning.

Two four-year-old girls, Maria and Ruby, hang up their coats and notice cookie trays on a table with magnetic alphabet letters in a basket. Ms. Curtis greets them, saying, "Good morning, girls! Ooh, do you see what I put out on our table this morning? Come look." The girls sit next to each other and pull a cookie tray close to them.

Ms. Curtis picks up the basket of alphabet letters and places it between the girls, saying, "Here are our alphabet letters. You can make your own words with these. You can make your name, big words, small words, or even a word with one letter!" The girls each dig into the basket of colorful letters and begin to feel the letters in their hands. Ms. Curtis steps back as the girls begin their explorations.

Maria: "Hey, my baby's gonna have a birthday."

Ruby: "Mine too. They need a birthday party. Let's bake a cake."

Both girls take letters one at a time from the basket and line up the letters across the top of their cookie sheets. Maria makes a row across the top and then down both sides. She is filling in the space from the outer edges toward the center. Ruby sticks to making lines of letters while pushing them tight against each other like puzzle pieces so they have as little space as possible between them.

Ruby then reaches over to a basket of pattern blocks on the nearby shelf, picks out small one-inch blue squares, and places them above her alphabet letters as decoration. Maria takes different colored shapes from the basket and decorates her alphabet cake with brown diamonds, red circles, and yellow hexagons.

After a few minutes, Ms. Curtis comes closer to their table and says, "Yum, you have an alphabet cake! Is there a message on your cakes with all those letters making words?"

Ruby says, "We bakin' cakes. My baby's havin a birthday."

Maria responds, "My baby is having the whole class come to her birthday. I'm making a big cake. All my cousins are coming too. We gotta bake a nice cake." The girls continue adding to their cakes for several more minutes.

With the image of Ms. Curtis and her children in mind, we now look at each of the five roles for teachers in the *Bridging* assessment process more closely.

Decision-Maker

The teacher and childcare provider's role as a decision-maker is particularly apparent before conducting the *Bridging* assessment. During the preparation phase, the teacher or provider:

▶ determines the windows of time for assessment during the school year;

▶ plans for how many children to assess at any one time and which activities to use; and

▶ locates opportunities to embed assessment activities in the daily routines, considering when and where to make activities available.

Teachers and childcare providers revisit the key concepts and skills embodied in the activity. Then, they identify the expected range of performance for children in the class as a starting point for observation. When making decisions, the teacher or provider draws on her knowledge of individual children, the activity's key concepts and skills, and ways in which the activity can invite the children's participation.

Ms. Curtis decided to assess each child's pretend play from late November through December. She set up her classroom with a tapestry of activities spread across the room. Ms. Curtis arrived early that morning to ensure that materials and furniture were set up and ready for the children's school day. Through quick coordination with her assistant, Ms. Curtis ensured a balance between supervision and assessment for the morning. As the children entered, put away their belongings, and eagerly found something interesting, Ms. Curtis spotted Ruby and Maria selecting the alphabet letters and cookie sheets table. She chose them as her assessment focus for the morning. With her watchful eye, Ms. Curtis monitored the classroom while focused on listening to the children's conversation and taking notes.

Unlike many traditional assessments that tell teachers and providers what to do and how to do it, *Bridging* depends on teachers and providers deciding what is best for their classroom and their children. *Bridging* invites teachers and providers to fully use their experience and expertise in decision-making to set the stage for children to engage in learning activities on their strongest footing.

In the case of Ms. Curtis's classroom, she had the activity and play areas set up so that they were conducive to small groups of children playing together. Her first allegiance was to support the children in good play and exploration; she did not manipulate play settings or redirect children to facilitate the assessment process. Instead, she seized a moment to collect assessment data as the opportunity arose. She did not start the day knowing exactly who she would observe or where she might position herself in the room. She started with one goal: to observe children in pretend play during the designated activity period. She made certain that children could engage with familiar play areas. She also planned for a new, yet simple, activity that might invite children's exploration: the magnetic letters for making words. When the girls saw the materials as an opportunity for pretend play, Ms. Curtis was right there, ready to listen and document what unfolded.

As classroom leaders, teachers, and childcare providers make decisions nonstop on any typical day, such as extending an activity for a longer time frame, rescheduling an activity for a later day, discontinuing an activity that is not working, or changing the order of activities to fit with how the day is going. Such flexibility – or "reading" of the children and the school day flow – is the cornerstone of teacher involvement in authentic assessment. *Bridging* asks teachers and providers to draw on the same decision-making skills they use in classroom teaching when making decisions about the assessment process.

Being flexible while using *Bridging's* assessment processes is not equivalent to having lax standards or no structure for the assessment process. Instead, *Bridging* gives teachers and providers authority and trusts them to follow best practice principles to guide their thinking and behavior during planning, implementation, and reflection on assessment findings. *Bridging* also assures teachers and providers that they are not stuck with the decisions they make. As with many aspects of daily activity in the classroom, they can adjust and update the plan with a more informed decision if something is not working or making sense. Tracking these decisions helps uncover the steps that make teaching and learning more effective.

Participant

As with the role of a decision-maker, the teacher and provider's role as an active participant in *Bridging* begins before the assessment starts. Specifically, teachers and childcare providers:

- ▶ organize materials for assessment activities; and

- ▶ review and understand key concepts and skills in various activities and their developmental progression.

The teacher and provider's role as a participant expands when interacting with children during the *Bridging* assessment process. Teachers and providers address logistical issues such as, "How will I introduce the activity in an inviting, playful way? How will I explain the goal of the activity to children? What concepts or steps in the task will I want to describe in some detail?" These are among the "how to" questions that call for providers' and teachers' decision-making to engage children effectively in the activity.

In the snapshot, Ms. Curtis set the stage for the children to start their school day. She set out cookie trays with magnetic letters to address the learning goal of children becoming familiar with the letters of the alphabet and the letter that starts their name. She was curious about how the children would take up her invitation to explore. She welcomed the girls and invited them to use the materials for the purpose she had in mind – making words. When the girls saw other possibilities for using the letters, Ms. Curtis was fine with that and open to seeing what would happen in their play. Her supportive, nonjudgmental approach to learning more about her children allowed her to observe their pretend play skills.

The children expected and were accustomed to their two teachers moving about the room, observing, encouraging their activity, and intervening to listen more closely if tension was in the air. When Ms. Curtis came close to the girls making birthday cakes, she commented on their activity, saying, "Yum, you have an alphabet cake! Is there a message on your cakes with all those letters making words?" The children responded to her on their own wavelength – making birthday cakes for their babies. Ms. Curtis was accepting and curious about how the children used the materials and setting.

Observer

Observation skills are among the most basic and critical skills of effective teachers and providers. They learn to see everything as if they "had eyes in the back of their heads" and to know what is happening in the classroom. *Bridging* recognizes that being a good observer – gathering information about children as individuals and as a group – is not a role reserved for moments of assessment. What a teacher or provider learns about a child from how the child walks into the room and engages with peers is as important as noticing how the child picks up a pencil to draw a picture during the *Bridging* assessment. Likewise, what a teacher or provider learns about the children from last week's picnic supper with families is also critical to the kinds of insights they will bring to bear on the analysis of *Bridging* assessment results. *Bridging* assessments depends on educators gathering and recording information on an ongoing basis and being able to keep relevant details in mind when interpreting a child's performance.

Ms. Curtis demonstrated her skill in listening closely in order to understand her children and follow the line of thought they developed. She watched how they responded to her comments without worrying about the gap between her wish to promote word-making and the girls' wish to make birthday cakes for their babies. The girls' response was developmentally appropriate, understandable, and even delightful! Ms. Curtis introduced the possibility of making words, and the girls were confident enough in their relationship with their teacher to respond honestly and thoughtfully. Their reaction also was their highest level of thinking in response to their teacher's invitation to engage in the activity. That was the goal – and their trust in their teacher allowed Ms. Curtis to capture their thinking.

In addition to observing children, the effective provider and teacher also observe the progress of the assessment process inside the day's curriculum implementation. The teacher or provider notes what is working well regarding logistics with this class of children and what needs to be changed or adjusted as the children progress. For example, the setup for materials, the space chosen for children to participate in an activity, and decisions about groupings of children are among the implementation decisions the teacher or provider makes and adjusts for as the day progresses.

As an observer, the teacher and provider watch and capture what children do when engaged in the *Bridging* assessment activities. This is when educators listen and observe closely to capture as much detail as possible. This is the heart of good assessment skills: observing and recording details without judging the child, but rather capturing the richness so that it can be studied when the children have left for the day. Guided by the key concepts and skills that the activity invites, the teacher or provider observes children's interaction with materials and performance in each activity. Based on these observations, the teacher or provider scores each child's performance, notes the child's reaction to task components such as social grouping, and records the child's working approaches. The teacher and provider also may note additional information, such as the child's comments or unexpected use of materials.

The primary responsibility of a teacher and provider is to carefully observe how each child responds to specific activity components. This role is especially important during the *Bridging* assessment process in order to gather authentic and accurate data to use when interpreting the child's behavior. A key factor in effectively gathering observational data lies in the teacher and provider's grasp of key concepts, skills, and diverse working approaches alongside recognizing the developmental progression of varied content knowledge.

Interpreter

As interpreters, teachers and providers make sense of the information they gather about children's performance. In the *Bridging* assessment process, teachers and providers review each child's profiles of performance scores and working approaches. They expect variability. Children respond to each task differently, they have favorites and preferences, and they have days when nothing feels right. In reviewing the data and considering the children's experiences, teachers and providers:

▶ score each child's performance and working approaches on each activity;

▶ look for patterns and relationships as well as identify each child's strengths and areas of inexperience or weakness; and

▶ identify the areas where children have achieved mastery and can work independently. They also pinpoint the skills and concepts children are currently developing and where children need further experience, targeted instruction, and/or time to make more progress.

In *Bridging*, teachers and providers understand the child's activity in a context that considers the characteristics of the task, the nature of the learning the child is doing, and the educator's insights about the child. Teachers and providers consider how different aspects of the assessment activity interact rather than attribute a child's performance to the effects of a single factor.

After Ms. Curtis observed her children's pretend play, she began the process of interpretation by looking at her observation notes related to the activity rubric. She looked first at three key aspects of the children's play: the children's use of materials, the nature of their talk, and how they related to each other. Next, she reviewed the rubric while considering to what extent the children created and explored a hypothetical situation they invented together using words and objects to represent aspects of the imaginary scene. Ms. Curtis recorded a Level 5 for both children. The two girls found each other as partners to build a story together – and they participated in building a story through emerging interactive play skills.

Ms. Curtis scored both girls as a 4 or 5 on each of the productive working approaches. Both children were eager to come to their chosen activity – they each formulated a goal, maintained their focus, and continued the play as they got further into baking and saw the possibilities with other materials nearby. For the descriptive working approaches, Ms. Curtis noted their chattiness as a central part of what sustained them both in play and exploration. In addition, they shared a narrative fantasy: making birthday cakes. They also worked at a comfortable, deliberate pace in synchrony with each other.

To support the data interpretation process, Table 4.2 provides questions about a child's activity performance and working approaches that teachers and providers can consider asking themselves. Although these questions are separated by category, we recognize that the content

Table 4.2 Reflection Questions for Interpreting the Assessment Results

Reflecting on a Child's Performance Levels

- What do I notice about the child's rubric scores across the five activities? Do the scores match what I sense this child is good at doing and what the child is drawn to doing?
- What comes to mind as I examine this child's performance levels? Does a pattern exist for the child's strengths and areas where the child has yet to develop?
- What activity goals, key concepts, and skills does the child understand? What are the strengths grounding this child? What does the child know and do confidently?
- What concepts and skills does the child seem to be working on in each curriculum area?
- What challenges the child? What seems to engage the child in a way that draws him or her into concentrating on working on a problem?
- How does the variability in the child's rubric scores compare to that of other children in the class?
- How might factors such as social grouping when working on an activity or activity materials influence the child's effort and performance score?
- If the child has participated in this activity before, how does the child's performance compare to previous experiences?

Reflecting on Working Approaches

- Is the child's working approach consistent across activities?
- How do the child's productive working approaches in areas of strength compare with those not as strong?
- How do the child's working approaches relate to their performance level?
- What does it mean when a child receives high working approach scores for an activity on which the child has a low rubric score?
- What does the information on working approaches suggest about how a child becomes productively engaged in school learning activities?

and process of learning variables do not work in isolation and are also interconnected when we attempt to interpret them. Teachers and providers will likely find themselves referencing both kinds of insight to understand assessment findings.

When reviewing and interpreting the assessment results, a teacher or provider compares the *Bridging* data with their knowledge of the children from observations in ongoing classroom activities because no one source of information provides a complete understanding of a child. Ms. Curtis has documentation on a rich sample of pretend play for the two children that she can refer to as she thinks about their progress in different learning areas. For example, she can compare their base of skills and their approach to engaging in play to what these same children do in counting collections, drawing a self-portrait, and acting out stories. Ms. Curtis is building a profile of what and how her children learn that looks at all children individually along with their ability to engage and grow from being with each other.

Equally important in the process of interpreting assessment findings is discussing findings and observations with other teachers and providers, the school principal or director, the child's parents, and even the child! Teachers, providers, and children have everything to gain as teachers and providers broaden their sources of insight. These insights include the child's performance of various activities and the knowledge of a variety of people who are committed to the child's learning and success in the classroom.

Cultural psychologists Michael Cole and Sylvia Scribner urged professionals to view assessment data as possibilities. By possibilities, they meant that assessment information can and ought to be regarded as "hypothesis generators," with data being interpreted from multiple points of view and used "as an opportunity to reexamine what good performance entails" (1974, p. 198). *Bridging* asks teachers and childcare providers to look at assessment results in terms of not only what a child does or does not know at any one moment but also what the child's performance *means* for them. The meaning that can be uncovered in patterns of assessment data becomes the story that the teacher can tell. The story embodies insights gathered from looking at the findings from various points of view. These perspectives include knowledge of individual children and the chemistry of how children learn together in this particular class. They also include the possible influences of task structure, materials, social arrangements, and the content area on a child's performance. Instead of attributing children's performance effects to a single dimension, *Bridging* invites teachers to consider how different dimensions of the assessment process interact constantly.

The meaning of *Bridging* assessment results cannot be set out and described in this book. Results are particular to individual children. Their meaning is relative to a specific educational context and is influenced by a child's family culture and community background. When interpreting the assessment results, teachers and providers will benefit enormously if they can work with colleagues because a rich interpretation of data takes patience and a willingness to consider various possible meanings and explanations.

Translator

The teacher and childcare provider's role as translator comes after the assessment activities have been completed. In the *Bridging* assessment process, being a translator involves:

- ▶ using the results to shape curriculum objectives, select materials, and design learning activities;

- ▶ identify points of entry for individual children in particular curriculum areas based on your assessment of what will best unlock their potential.

The translation begins when teachers and providers ask themselves questions, such as, "What are my priorities for learning and teaching given the assessment findings from today? What will I focus on tomorrow and in the upcoming weeks? How can I align my instructional methods with what I learned from the assessment process?"

When looking for entry points for each child to reach new goals, teachers and providers can ask themselves questions, such as, "How can a child's interests become an entry point to a curriculum area where the child has little experience? Which of our *Bridging* tasks this week did children find easy, and which were harder?" The teacher or provider might engage the children in a conversation about what their strengths are, what areas are difficult, and what the child's interests are at school. Such discussions have no right or wrong answers. These conversations only provide more opportunities for group and individual awareness. Information the children provide might help the teacher better understand the assessment results and gain new insights into how to translate them into learning experiences for the children.

Ms. Curtis made a few notes after observing the children's play with the materials she had set out for the activity that reflected the following insights:

- ▶ The children responded well to the classroom setup which invited small groups of children to interact. Ms. Curtis was mindful of what materials and activities were adjacent and how they were spaced in the classroom.

- ▶ The materials that involved a lot of small pieces were used appropriately and constructively. Since the end of October, Ms. Curtis had been slowly introducing new material each week, explaining how they might be used and how to take good care of them in the classroom.

⬧ Currently, the children's exploration concentrated on the physical properties of materials, which Ms. Curtis believed was a crucial foundation for the later abstract use of these materials. She will continue to observe their material exploration and ensure that it's integrated into the learning process. For instance, she noticed the children watching her incorporate alphabet letters into various activities throughout the school day. By introducing magnetic letters for play, she aims to familiarize the children with a new dimension of using letters in their play and conversations. In the coming months, the alphabet – coupled with the children's vibrant imaginations – will form the cornerstone of their emergent writing and reading development.

Regarding interactions among the children, Ms. Curtis saw that these two girls were confident and assertive in participating in their play activity. They also brought their imagination and wish to connect with others verbally into their play. Ms. Curtis watched for these qualities because they signal a healthy classroom climate for children to test their thinking, experiment with possible ideas, and know they are being heard.

Figure 4.1 depicts the dynamic flow of the five integral roles a teacher and provider assume within the *Bridging* assessment process. It is important to note that while we delineate these teacher and provider roles sequentially – before, during, and after assessment – they remain fluid and adaptable in a real-world application. They flexibly respond to the nuances of assessment activities, individual student engagements, and group dynamics at any given juncture. Teachers and providers frequently embody multiple roles concurrently throughout the *Bridging* assessment

Figure 4.1   The Dynamic Flow of the Five Teacher/Childcare Provider Roles in *Bridging* Assessment

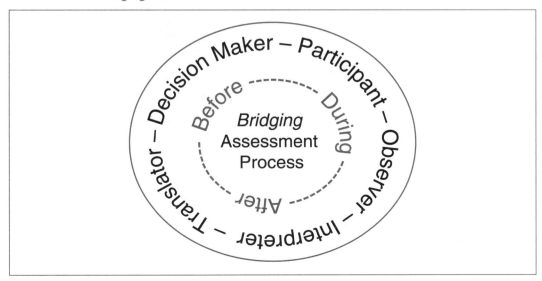

process. Ultimately, teachers and providers hold the reins in the *Bridging* assessment process by exploring these five pivotal questions:

> ◗ **Decision-maker:** How will I use *Bridging* in my classroom at different points in the school year?

> ◗ **Participant:** What concepts and skills embedded in the *Bridging* activity require my attention when facilitating the assessment and children's learning?

> ◗ **Observer:** What do I notice children doing? What concepts, skills, and working approaches are evident in each child's efforts?

> ◗ **Interpreter:** What do results from each activity and across activities suggest about each child's learning, and the group's progress?

> ◗ **Translator:** How can I use results to further children's learning and development in the upcoming days and weeks?

Our intention in outlining these roles is not to establish rigid boundaries, but rather to illuminate the distinctive facets intrinsic to each dimension of professional teaching. This perspective sheds light on the assessment process, instructional strategizing, and the intricate interplay of these roles within the realm of proficient teaching. At the core of the *Bridging* assessment paradigm lies the empowerment and involvement of teachers and childcare providers.

Bridging and Effective Teaching

CHAPTER #5

Psychologist L. S. Vygotsky once compared the work of educators to that of farmers. Effective farmers do not gauge the health and progress of plants under their care based only on the harvest at the end of the growing season. Instead, they are aware of and monitor the growing plants at every step, from planting the seeds to the appearance of the fruit. Farmers demonstrate their skills by carefully observing crops for signs of change throughout the growing season. They also keep mental notes on factors contributing to or hindering growth — such as the amount of sunlight, rain, and nutrients in the soil. Reviewing and interpreting sources of information also helps farmers determine when interventions are needed to support and sustain growth that will deliver a healthy harvest.

Similarly, effective teachers and childcare providers plan learning experiences based on more than what children have completed or mastered in the classroom on any one day. Effective teachers and childcare providers observe children's involvement in activities in the present in relation to patterns of learning that have led up to today, with an eye toward the children's future. They continuously seek to articulate what concepts and skills their children are working on and how children's development will likely proceed in the upcoming days and weeks. Effective teachers and providers stay alert to the support, guidance, and adjustments children need to further their learning. When teachers and providers organize a day for children engaged in activities that open the door to new learning at the moment and in the near future, the teacher and the children are having a good day in school.

Bridging offers a way to harmonize the many seemingly conflicting responsibilities that teachers and providers face: teaching *and* assessment. In the *Bridging* approach, these two processes intertwine, with assessment serving as a catalyst for effective teaching within early childhood classroom environments. This chapter includes an extended snapshot of Mrs. Martinez's kindergarten classroom showing a piece of *Bridging* assessment process at work inside her well-developed classroom structure and routines. This snapshot illustrates how *Bridging* empowers teachers and providers to conduct as assessment while seamlessly nurturing children's daily growth and learning.

Classroom Snapshot: Mrs. Martinez and Her Kindergarteners

Beginning the Day. Mrs. Martinez is a kindergarten teacher with 27 children from a diverse urban neighborhood. Parents and older children drop their five-year-olds off in the playground; the sounds of several different languages can be heard around the yard. Then, when the bell rings, the children line up by the door in front of their teacher, whom they now recognize readily in the fourth week of school. The children come through the school door with a burst of energy; the sky is deep blue, the air is crisp and bright, and the fall day has the group starting out full of excitement and on a good footing.

Mrs. Martinez greets her children at the doorway. Then she invites them to pick up their breakfast trays and go to their seats for time to eat and chat. As children finish breakfast, Mrs. Martinez guides them in cleaning up. She instructs them to go to the rug to look at a book with a friend while they wait for the group to be ready for the morning meeting. Yesterday, Mrs. Martinez talked with the children about how to look at a book with a friend. She recognizes that every detail of the school day is new to her children. Learning the routines of getting along with another child or a large group of peers in a friendly and cooperative way are skills the children need to become aware of and practice. Kindergarten is full of beginnings and learning new skills for the first time.

Building Community. Mrs. Martinez begins the morning meeting with a song, "Make New Friends." The children have picked up the two simple verses. Today, Mrs. Martinez will lead the group in singing the song as a round with the help of her student teacher, Ms. Johnson. The skills in singing a song in unison and harmony exemplify the goals Mrs. Martinez has for her class. She wants to help her children feel they belong to a caring community in which rich learning activities occur in a collaborative context of giving and receiving help. She also wants them to find new challenges and experiences inviting so they will want to come back and do more with others every day.

Stories, Discussion, and Acting. Today Mrs. Martinez reads one of her favorite Leo Leoni books to the group, *Fish Is Fish*. When she is done, she guides the group in acting out the story, with half of the children playing the fish and half of the group acting out the role of the tadpole. Lots of motion and excitement occur as the fish and tadpole have an outing in the water and then briefly on land. When the scene is complete, Mrs. Martinez invites the actors to sit on the edge of the rug. She follows up with, "Children, I have a question for you. At the end of the story, Fish says, 'You were right. Fish is Fish'. What was Frog right about? What does it mean that 'fish is fish'?"

Antonio responds:	"The fish can't do everything. It does what a fish does."
Mrs. Martinez echoes:	"It does what a fish does. Who else can put this into words, what it means: 'fish is fish'?"
Gabriella says:	"Frog looked like a fish when she was little so she thought she was a fish. 'Is she a fish'?"

After three to four minutes of discussion, Mrs. Martinez tells the group, "I have two more short stories to read to you that we will act out today. These stories are ones children told last year when they were in this classroom. Listen to this." Mrs. Martinez shows the group a small piece of paper with a few words written on it. "Here is a story one boy told: 'Once there was a shark with a big eye. There was a seahorse who went hopping. The eye went up to the seahorse, then Nemo, then a dolphin. It got the dolphin.'"

Mrs. Martinez then says, "Now we will act it out. I want you all to sit on the edge of our rug. The rug is our stage. I will ask you if you want to play a part. You can say 'Yes' and stand on the stage or say 'No'. If you say no, I will move to the next person to see if you want to play that part." Mrs. Martinez then addresses the child next to her and asks, "Would you like to be the shark?" She proceeds around the edge of the circle, asking if the next child wants to be the seahorse, then Nemo, and then the dolphin. She tells the children that actors pretend. That means "no touching" anyone else. She guides the children in enacting this ocean story.

Mrs. Martinez then reads the second story. "Now here is a story a girl told last year. 'One princess and one baby and one castle and one prince. The monster tear down the castle. He drag out the princess and the prince rescue the princess.'" She recruits the next four children on the edge of the rug to play the parts of the princess, prince, baby, and monster. She offers parts to children regardless of whether they are a boy or a girl. The focus is on the character that needs to be portrayed. Everyone will have an opportunity to play a role if they choose.

Group time is coming to a close. Mrs. Martinez tells the class that she will make sure everyone gets a chance to tell a story over the next few days. She adds that she will write their stories down just as she did with the shark story as well as the prince and princess story. Then the class will act out the stories they dictate.

Making Choices. "Today, we will start the day with choice time," Mrs. Martinez says. "Your job is to look around our classroom and pick a good activity to do. You can choose:

- building with blocks on our block rug;

- working at the painting/drawing/writing table (where stencils of alphabet letters are laid out for the children to explore and use);

- playing in the house area; or

- picking a puzzle or game from our shelf to play on one of the tables by the window."

Mrs. Martinez continues, "Your job now is to pick a good activity. This past week, we have been talking about how we do this. What do you remember about picking a good activity? What might you think right now as you wonder what to do next? You might be thinking. . ." Mrs. Martinez now points to a chart with the label "Choosing" on it. It also has icons symbolizing different ways children might make their choice. She reviews the chart with the group and explains the meaning of each icon with the following words:

- **Interesting (picture of a child wondering about something):** "Maybe there is something out on a table that looks exciting, interesting, something we want to try."

- **Friend (picture of two children laughing together):** "I want to play with my friend. Friends often have good ideas we want to listen to and explore together."

- **New (picture of a child with a big, surprised look on his face):** "I see something new that I have never done before, and I want to find out how it works."

- **Not finished (picture of a child building an elaborate structure with blocks):** "I want to return to the activity I didn't finish yesterday and work on it more today."

Today's "Bluelight Special." Mrs. Martinez has told the children about her family's favorite department store, Kmart, in the neighborhood where she grew up. The counters around the store had items on display near light poles with blue lightbulbs. While shopping, customers would hear announcements about a "Bluelight Special" at a particular counter. People could look around the store and see the blue light flashing. It meant "This is where the action is" for that item at a good price. In her classroom, Mrs. Martinez tells the children that when she has a special activity for the day, she will feature it at a central table where she keeps a lamp with a blue lightbulb. Each child will be invited to participate in the activity sometime during the day. Everyone will get a turn with the Bluelight Special.

Mrs. Martinez adds, "Today, everyone will try the activity Counting Collections. You will work with Ms. Johnson at our Bluelight Special table. Ms. Johnson has several bags of materials for you to investigate. She will keep track of who has had a turn and invite you over if you have not had a turn by the end of the morning. Ms. Johnson is standing by the table where the bags of the new collection are waiting." Ms. Johnson holds up several baggies of small items and says, "Good morning, children. I'm here at the collections table, and here are the bags. Come for your turn, or I'll call you over sometime today."

Mrs. Martinez continues, "Let's start with children who want to work with Ms. Johnson on Counting Collection*s*. Who's ready to go with her to that table? Ms. Johnson wants four children right now."

During the first 40 minutes of the school day, Mrs. Martinez incorporates three out of the five *Bridging* activities into the daily schedule. She includes imaginative pretend play, learning about dictating a story and acting it out, and working with Ms. Johnson on counting collections. These activities are thoughtfully integrated into the daily routine – a testament to their seamless fit and inherent value for both Mrs. Martinez and her students. Instead of requiring that teachers evaluate children's learning using separate assessments, *Bridging* provides activities that teachers and childcare providers weave harmoniously into the educational fabric of the school day. These assessment activities coexist unobtrusively with Mrs. Martinez's teaching endeavors, while the children actively engage and learn.

All teachers and providers also learn – and continue to learn. But two critical activities make strong professional teaching possible and set the stage for it to continue to improve: reviewing and thinking about the details of teaching and then doing so with colleagues. In the snapshot, Mrs. Martinez offers us a wealth of information about her teaching. She also provides many examples of how she values the children's thinking and supports it in every step of the day. After this activity, Mrs. Martinez now has valuable additional details on which to reflect. How will Mrs. Martinez use the information she gathered from this morning in school? All teachers learn and continue to learn. What professional supports make her learning possible? What professional supports will make further learning possible?

Bridging and Teacher Reflective Practice

Bridging is designed with teachers' professional development needs in mind. Becoming proficient in teaching is a developmental process. The literature acknowledges that learning to teach – and to assess children's learning – takes time. Experience is the best teacher after the initial preparation of coursework and student teaching. However, experience alone does not help teachers develop more effective practice. Teachers must also reflect on, discuss, debate, and rethink their teaching practice. Learning to teach well is a lifelong endeavor; good teachers are not afraid to say that their learning is never complete, and that they are always working to improve their practice.

Reflective practice is integral to the *Bridging* assessment process because it seamlessly connects assessment with teaching. When reviewing the assessment results across activities, teachers and providers cannot help but think of the curriculum instruction contributing to children's learning profiles. This reflective practice enables teachers and providers to gain insights from what happened in order to improve future work. In Tables 5.1 and 5.2, we suggest a set of reflection questions related to the teacher and childcare provider's role in assessing children as well as specific *Bridging* assessment tasks and processes. These questions

Table 5.1   Reflective Questions on General Classroom Assessment

1. What professional or personal experiences changed your teaching approach, "stopping you in your tracks" and leading you in a new direction?
2. What are the best ways to gather insights about what children know and can do?
3. How have your classroom assessment experiences influenced your teaching?
4. Which kind of activity is most helpful to capture students' strengths and interests?
5. How does our perspective shift when we assess what and how children are learning in order to better understand children rather than judge their performance?
6. What classroom environment is conducive or necessary for performance assessment?
7. How does active participation in teaching and assessment affect your thinking about the assessment process and results?

Table 5.2   Reflective Questions on *Bridging* Assessment

1. Which *Bridging* content areas are your areas of strength? Which areas require you to work hard to see the knowledge and skills involved?
2. What surprises you when tracking children's productive and descriptive working approaches? Which approaches are comfortable for you, and which require you to become more flexible and open-minded (for example, regarding children's chattiness)?
3. Choose two children who puzzle or challenge you. What do you learn about each child in the context of *Bridging* activities? Is the child at his or her best in one particular activity? What is it about the activity that engages the child – the setup, the materials, the content, or the peer interactions?
4. What do you notice when looking at an individual child's profile?
   a. Where do surprising differences exist?
   b. What does performance variability suggest?
   c. What do changes in working approaches on different *Bridging* tasks suggest?
   d. What might be contributing to working approach variability?
5. What do you notice about your children as a group when you look at the class performance levels across the five *Bridging* content areas? Could some areas benefit from a change in set-up, scheduling, or materials used?
6. Plan to visit a colleague's classroom when *Bridging* activities are being implemented. What details stand out about how your colleague sees and presents the activity? What is striking to you about seeing other teachers' children carrying out *Bridging* activities?

provide starting points for preservice and in-service educators to think about effective teaching to support their children's learning across the early childhood years.

Bridging and Teacher Collaboration

The ideas presented in this book can certainly be read and used by individual educators. But the benefits expand when used by teachers and childcare providers working together regularly over the school year in preservice education or as part of professional development for early childhood educators in a center or a school. As with children, teachers and providers grow from interactions with their peers when they can review and study their teaching in a supportive and responsive setting. Teacher educators can help teachers and providers become better professionals by providing a structure for them to discuss their work. *Bridging* offers such a structure.

Teachers and providers inevitably have many questions when reviewing assessment data as they try to make sense of what children are thinking and how to best support children's next steps. They need to reconsider many details daily in order to adjust the schedule to maximize learning in different curricular areas for small and large groups of children. Teachers and providers benefit from advice, modeling, and coaching from their colleagues. Peer collaboration with a shared goal and common thread of activities helps form a community of learners in which colleagues are some of the providers' and teachers' greatest sources of support.

Bridging can further help teachers and providers broaden and deepen their discussions of children's learning and the teaching process while working with their colleagues. Teachers and providers do not learn these skills once during initial preparation and then proceed for years without further discourse with other professionals. Teachers hone their skills through years of experience and dialogue with other professionals. Teachers need time to try out ideas and discuss their initial efforts with others. They also need to practice such skills as how to word questions or rethink how they introduce an activity to children.

Bridges to Effective Teaching

Effective teaching is engaged teaching, resulting in joyful learning. Lee Schulman is the past president of the American Educational Research Association and the Carnegie Foundation for the Advancement of Teaching. Schulman once defined effective teaching as the coalescence of three categories of knowledge: (1) knowledge of the content area being taught, (2) knowledge of students and their thinking and learning as a group and individually, and (3) a repertoire of teaching methods appropriate for the subject matter and the needs of students (Shulman, 1986, 1987). Each area of knowledge embodies rich and complex thinking and skills, which teachers may spend a lifetime developing.

Moving from assessment to curriculum, *Bridging* makes visible the three types of knowledge deemed essential to effective teaching by Shulman: the key concepts and skills of content areas, the developmental status of the children manifested through *Bridging* assessment activities, and teaching methods that can incorporate the assessment results into plans for future activities. *Bridging* operationalizes and integrates these three sources of effective teaching through assessment activities for teaching and learning. The assessment process and the teacher's thinking are integrated into effective teaching practices.

The *Bridging* assessment process seeks a continuous flow of thinking on the part of teachers and providers as they engage children in *Bridging* activities. These activities become a prototype for the kind of disciplined thinking effective teachers and providers do to update instruction based on the feedback they gather on each child as the class moves ahead. The teacher or provider adjusts the daily challenges children meet and the discourse connecting all participants over time. The *Bridging* assessment provides a road map for this complex unfolding work.

We chose the name *Bridging* for this educational assessment to emphasize its dynamic nature and the sequential actions involved in constructing bridges. Numerous pivotal components must harmonize to achieve success in the education of young children. The framework and methodology of *Bridging* provide a scaffold for assisting early childhood educators in constructing bridges between:

- ▶ routine instructional activities and continuous classroom assessment practices;

- ▶ children's funds of knowledge from their homes and communities and the new intellectual demands of schooling;

- ▶ the content and process of children's learning;

- ▶ children's current learning progress and their future developmental paths within and across curricular areas;

- ▶ key concepts and skills in foundational school subject areas and children's adeptness in mastering this foundational knowledge;

- ▶ the assessment results and the refined curriculum planning and execution.

This endeavor of building bridges is intricate, with teachers and childcare providers playing a pivotal role in the process. The ultimate objective of *Bridging* is to empower educators to recognize and address the diverse needs of each child, fostering their growth within the interconnected and mutually influential realms of assessment and teaching.

SECTION II
BRIDGING ASSESSMENT ACTIVITIES

Pretend Play

- Significance of Pretend Play in Childcare and School

- Key Concepts and Skills in Pretend Play

- Conducting the Assessment

- Classroom Snapshot: Ms. Curtis and Her Preschoolers

- *Bridging* Assessment to Teaching

Pretend play is a form of voluntary activity in which young children take on imaginary roles while creating and imitating actions, gestures, and the talk of the characters they are imagining. In its most fully developed form, pretend play in childcare and school is intellectual, cognitive, verbal, and it is social – involving collaboration with at least one other person. In such play, the emphasis is on children working together to coordinate the roles and actions of various characters within an imaginary scene. Together, children create a story with problems and resolutions that ebb and flow as the children sustain interaction with one another inside the evolving storyline. In pretend play, children engage in discussion about people, circumstances, and possibilities for how the story will unfold. Pretend play with others requires flexibility in thinking, creativity, and imagination. While pretending, children generate imaginary possibilities, and then they speak and act while synthesizing the points of view of other children and the characters they are role playing.

It is important to include pretend play in childcare settings and in school in the flow of teaching and learning activities because it is the ultimate integrated inclusive curriculum under the leadership of a childcare provider or teacher who is aware and alert to its key role in children's learning. Pretend play has several parts:

1. The childcare provider or teacher prepares the environment with materials that lend themselves to children using them in multiple ways while pretending and allots a minimum of 45 minutes for children to make choices among the activities available.

2. Children use the space, time, and materials to pretend. They create stories and role play characters with their plots and problems.

3. The teacher or provider listens and observes carefully to help facilitate the children's play, particularly when there are upset moments and children need assistance getting imaginary scenes moving forward again.

Significance of Pretend Play in Childcare and School

People may ask, why are we making time for pretend play in childcare and school when children have time to play at home or in their neighborhood? It is essential in childcare and school because pretend play embodies children's highest level of abstract logical thinking. Children gravitate toward the chance to pretend – they seek out activities that invite imagination, utilize their creative impulses. Children bring their best selves to making pretend play work. There are many important benefits to grounding early childhood curriculum in opportunities for pretend play in childcare centers and schools.

- **Pretend play is thinking.** It is the place where young children create and articulate problems, compile and integrate new ideas into their awareness, and in the process of playing, they review, extend, and build deeper understandings of how people, situations, and materials work together to solve problems. Pretend play embodies the essential goals of schooling: that each child's world opens to new possibilities – ideas, problems, activities, skills, and resources to meet the future alongside others. That is what builds a society of professionals who are ready to address future problems collaboratively.

- **Pretend play is symbolic activity.** The problems and their resolution that children focus on are not derived from the immediate here and now circumstances but rather are problems that are hypothetical, imaginary. In pretend play, children more readily observe, define, and manipulate the parts and roles being enacted. Pretend play creates a laboratory for practicing the skills of solving dilemmas inside daily experiences.

- **Pretend play is verbal.** Pretend play is imaginary and therefore requires verbal language. Children speak and listen to each other as they discuss the premises of a story problem, who is involved, and the roles different characters fill.

- **Pretend play is social.** When playing with others, children experience how the group can accomplish more than any one individual could alone. It addresses a 21st century learning goal:

learning how to solve problems collaboratively. Together, children learn how to use their knowledge and skills to foster the well-being of the group.

▶ **Pretend play is emotional.** Children care deeply about new ideas and about being creative, lively, humorous, and even generous while working and making friends. Pretend play is the one context that holds opportunities for children to experience frustration, disappointment, and disagreement in a safe and manageable way while they learn to regulate and modulate their emotional resources alongside ideas they care about in an integrated satisfying productive way.

Key Concepts and Skills in Pretend Play

Pretend play is necessary in the balancing of child-initiated and teacher-guided experiences in school and childcare learning. It provides the time and space for the give and take of listening and speaking between and among teachers, providers, and children. The key concepts and skills children develop in pretend play include:

▶ **Language.** Children learn to speak and listen in order to express ideas and pursue goals.

▶ **Thinking and reasoning.** Children learn to consider possibilities by examining hypothetical problems, their premises, and the situations where they arise.

▶ **Symbolic play.** Children learn to use objects in the environment to represent aspects of the imaginary world being created.

▶ **Social and interpersonal skills.** Children learn tolerance and consideration of others while negotiating to achieve a shared understanding of a situation.

▶ **Conflict management.** Children learn to handle disagreements and the emotions generated when participating in the give-and-take process of developing story ideas.

Conducting the Assessment

For preschool and kindergarten-aged children, school and childcare settings can begin the school year with a sampling of the following pretend play areas. Providers and teachers can introduce new areas as children learn to use the materials and understand how to play with many children in a variety of designated areas.

Materials. Childcare, preschool, and kindergarten classrooms will want to include areas with wooden building blocks (unit blocks) and an area that reflects household settings such as kitchen and sleeping area (small table, chairs, cabinet, doll bed) and includes the following kinds of objects:

▶ Scarves, hats, handbags, and pieces of cloth of various colors that can be used for different purposes such as blankets, clothing, rug, and a cape;

▶ Dolls reflecting a variety of ethnicities;

▶ Small figurines of people, animals, and vehicles;

▶ Small objects in baskets that children can use flexibly as their imaginations dictate such as wooden spools, chopsticks, popsicle sticks, and large buttons.

For preschool, kindergarten, and childcare, the setting will include:

▶ A drawing/writing table with materials easily reached including paper, crayons, markers, paper of various sizes and colors, scissors, rulers, tape, and stapler;

▶ An area for small manipulatives such as pattern blocks, unifix cubes, Lego, and wooden beads for stringing;

▶ Art areas for wet work (painting) and dry work (clay, collage work, making things with paper, cardboard);

▶ Sand and/or water tables with spoons, funnels, cups, small figures of people and animals;

▶ A space for games such as card games, board games, and puzzles;

▶ A classroom library/book area with places to sit comfortably and read books alone or with a friend.

Time. Full-day childcare, preschool, and kindergarten classrooms do well to have a minimum of two 45+ minute periods of continuous uninterrupted time for children to choose activities and engage with the materials in the various areas of the room. Play during a day of assessment observation will be no different than play on any other day. The teacher or provider will signal the beginning of the play period and maintain the usual role of oversight and interest in what the children choose to do while giving reminders about rules as necessary.

Rules. The first six weeks of childcare and school are an important time for creating the rhythms and expectations for this time period. Of primary importance is the safety of all. Ground rules that create a safe environment for all include:

1. **Safety** – No hurting others physically or emotionally.

2. **No exclusion** of any kind – The materials and the people in the classroom are there to benefit the group. No one is left out, and

each child's learning is the responsibility of everyone in the group. No one can say, "You can't play" (Paley, 1990).

3. **Talking** out all disagreements – Discussion and negotiation of upset situations is the procedure until an agreement is achieved. Childcare providers, teachers, and children repair breakdowns in play scenarios by asking, "What role are you trying to play?" "What could your character say in this situation?" "How can you adjust the story line so that it fits in this space, in this moment with others, and given the materials we have?"

4. **Each child's problem is everyone else's business** – Everyone in the group is responsible for helping good activities move forward by reminding others of the rules and agreements that the group has developed and calling upon the provider or teacher for help as needed.

Childcare Provider and Teacher's Role – For the children who are the focus of assessment, providers and teachers observe the child's activity during the play period. Providers and teachers focus on two to four children in one observation time frame. While observing, they note the following characteristics in the child's play on the recording sheet along with the child's working approach:

▶ **Objects:** Is a child using an object in a make-believe way, using an object such as a wooden block to represent a helicopter or spaceship dock, a bed, or a lion?

▶ **Movement and gestures:** Gestures and movements that are an imitation of the character they are portraying such as being a mother, a space captain, or someone other than themselves.

▶ **Language:** Words mark the creating of a make-believe situation such as, "Pretend you are a baby lion and you are lost and I am looking for you..."

▶ **Collaboration:** Nature of verbal interactions with others:

  – talk in the role of a character;

  – talk that contributes to the negotiation of who's who and what's happening in the play scenario;

  – talk that intervenes among conflicting parties to bring resolution to differences in point of view.

To what extent are there signs of the children jointly collaborating in constructing a pretend scenario?

▶ **Time in play:** Length of time children are engaged in play.

At the end of the play session, the provider or teacher assigns a rubric score and working approach scores for the level that is most representative of the child's activity during that period of time.

Classroom Snapshot: Ms. Curtis and Her Preschoolers

In Chapter 4, we met Ms. Curtis, a preschool teacher, starting her school day with the chance to observe two children, Maria and Ruby, in pretend play with new materials she set out for the day: magnetic alphabet letters placed on metal cookie sheets. As the two girls were making pretend birthday cakes for their babies, two boys came along to work with other materials at the same table. When Lawrence and Marco sat at the table next to the girls and began playing with peg boards, Ms. Curtis realized that she could readily include them in her observation of pretend play. In the end, Ms. Curtis collected data on all four children's pretend play: Ruby, Maria, Lawrence, and Marco. Here are Ms. Curtis' observations that continue from where we left off in Chapter 4.

While Ruby and Maria continue to carefully place pattern blocks over most of the alphabet letters, classmates Marco and Lawrence bring peg boards and pegs to the other end of the table near the girls. The boys also bring a basket of small plastic counting bears that they are going to put in cages. The two boys then push their peg boards together to make one larger surface and then get bears and pegs in hand.

Marco puts two bears on the board and starts to put pegs around them. Lawrence starts lining up pegs using all green pegs first, then a line of yellow pegs and then a line of red ones. He says, "Let's make cages and put a daddy and a baby bear in each." Marco takes a handful of bears and lines them up between the rows of pegs that Lawrence is creating.

Marco says, "These are the bad guys. They're going to jail. They don't get a birthday. No birthday cake for them." The boys overhear Maria and Ruby discussing cake baking. Marco says to Ruby, "We've got the bad guys. We won't let them out for the party."

Ruby responds, "OK, give me the cousins who can come to the party."

Marco gives her a handful of the smallest counting bears and says, "Here are the babies. They can eat cake."

Maria:	"Hey, we need those candles you got!" She points to the pegs.
Ruby:	"Hey, I'm going to put sprinkles on my cake." She grabs a pile of pegs from the basket by Lawrence.
Lawrence:	"Hey, those are mine! No touching my grenades!"
Ruby:	"I need some. You have too many. Give me the orange ones." Ruby can see orange pegs in the basket that Lawrence hasn't touched yet.

Lawrence picks out a handful and gives them to Ruby. He says, "My guys are going to blast off now to go fight the scorpions. They'll take their ammo to the spaceship."

There is a deck of cards at the end of the table that the teacher had given to several children for playing "Old Maid" by matching two cards that look alike. The children had finished, and Lawrence now gets an idea on seeing them. He grabs some cards and places them on top of the pegs making a sort of roof over the counting bears on the peg boards. Then he places some counting bears on top of the cards and says, "They're gonna launch into space here and get the bad guys."

Soon, the birthday cakes are cooking with alphabet letters, pattern block shapes, pegs as sprinkles, and bears lined up on the outside edges of the cookie sheets ready to eat. Preparations for the party are progressing and the bad guys are nowhere near the babies; they're in space.

Ruby:	"My baby wants her birthday food. She want tacos, nachos and potato chips and cupcakes."
Maria:	"My baby says, 'I love mommy.' Then she say, 'Run baby, run.' Then I tell her, 'Jump, Baby, jump!'"

Ms. Curtis rings her chime and tells the children it's time to clean up for their outdoor time. She says, "For those playing at the table here, leave everything just as it is. You have made beautiful birthday cakes and a spaceship for the bad guys. Let others look at them, and then we will do clean up later."

Ms. Curtis recognizes that the cookie trays and peg boards filled with bears, pegs, pattern blocks, magnetic letters, and plastic playing cards could create a daunting mess if she tried to get them sorted out and put them away at this time. She plans to create an activity after lunch where she sets out paper cups on the table and assigns small groups of children to visit the table for a few minutes each to sort objects into the paper cups and then dump them into the larger bins designated for bears, pegs, and alphabet letters. She has developed this system to turn a messy clean-up time into a productive sorting of objects ready for a new day of play tomorrow. Her decision is brilliant! She took a moment that could generate anxiety and uncertainty for four-year-olds and simplified it so that the class could transition from a deeply engrossing play scenario to outdoor time as a group. Ms. Curtis saw an opening for this clean-up task to connect children with other curriculum goals: sorting and classifying objects central to mathematics and science learning goals.

Ms. Curtis scored Maria and Ruby at a Level 5 of Pretend Play signaling Interactive Play skills that are developing well. She scored Lawrence and Marco at the same level. Ms. Curtis also noted that she saw evidence of Level 6 opening up for the children: the two pairs of children began to connect their stories when the boys kept bad guys away from the girls' birthday celebrations for their babies. They also handled the issue of sharing pegs well when there was a moment of feeling someone wasn't sharing fairly. Ms. Curtis was aware that these are skills that are developing and within reach for these children. To be in preschool with skills at Level 5 and approaching Level 6 means that the children will be able to spend their kindergarten year in "the graduate school of pretend play" (Paley, 2004), the place where they can practice, expand, and deepen their skills in imaginative thinking, problem-solving, negotiating and collaborating with peers, and resolving conflicts. All of these talents are included in 21st century learning goals.

For the boys' working approaches, she scored both boys at a Level 4 on the productive Working approaches. Both boys were helpful to each other in getting the materials they needed, with one minor uncertainty resolved readily. Ms. Curtis noted that for the Cooperation continuum, it was Lawrence who showed a tendency to be the one to step up to help others.

Ms. Curtis took from this observation period the goal to address how children help one another and share materials in classroom activities. These are skills she wants the children to have more fully developed by the time they leave her classroom – the knowledge that they can count on their own needs getting met, and that they can invest in helping others get their needs met also.

Bridging Assessment to Teaching

All forms of play (imitation, dramatic, or pretend) are universal forms of human activity that are shaped by social and cultural influences. Learning to play begins with the potential that all babies worldwide are born with and that is shaped by patterns of activity and conversation in local settings. Much of how young children learn to play is influenced by daily interaction with peers as Vivian Paley eloquently describes in the quote here.

If, in the world of fantasy play, four- and five-year-olds may be called characters in search of a plot, then the three-year-old is surely a character in search of a character. Place this three-year-old in a room of other threes, and sooner or later they will become an acting company. Should there happen to be a number of somewhat older peers about to offer stage directions and dialogue, the metamorphosis will come sooner rather than later. The dramatic images that flutter through their minds, as so many unbound stream-of-consciousness novels, begin to emerge as audible scripts to be performed on demand. (Paley, 1986, p. xiv)

The childcare, preschool, and kindergarten years are prime time for this awakening of children's imagination in relation to others in this new dynamic setting called a classroom. Imagination is essential for all future learning. It is the childcare provider and teacher's job to understand its importance, how to nurture its growth, and how to harness children's imagination to support school learning goals.

Many providers and teachers assume that "play is a child's work," that it is not the adult's place to become involved in children's play.

Providers and teachers let children decide what they will do and hope that they will do so productively. This is a good starting point, but more is needed from providers and teachers for pretend play to become a valuable learning opportunity. We advocate for a more assertive and intentional role for providers and teachers in relation to the children's imaginative play. Pretend play is a powerful force in children's learning *when* providers and teachers hold in mind the goal for pretend play in childcare and school and guide children toward that goal under careful supervision. As with all aspects of childcare and schooling, children need to learn how pretend play works outside of their home.

We believe that it is not the provider or teacher's role to decide the content of children's pretend play, or to even require that a child participate in it. The provider and teacher's main job is to create the conditions for good play to unfold, help children get started, and know how to intervene to restore the flow of pretend play when children fall into an argument, get stuck, want to exclude others, or become upset and are unable to use words to explain themselves and get their story back on track. We can see Ms. Curtis carrying out this role as she prepared her classroom for the morning of play in November, and then stayed attentive as she watched the children enter the room and take up the invitation to explore, create, and build with others.

Having said this, we also want to acknowledge that in some cultures, teachers and providers *do* participate in pretend play with their children and readily support and enhance the imagination young children are pursuing in their story. For example, Chinese early childhood educators readily enter into children's pretend play as a participant in the unfolding story such as being a patient in the hospital or a shopper in the grocery store (Tobin et al., 2009). However, for this kind of participatory role in pretend play to benefit children, it is important that teachers and providers resist the urge to turn pretend play into a lesson focused on skills that might be of concern to the teacher such as labeling objects, naming colors, and reciting counting numbers correctly. When the provider or teacher joins the activity as a player rather than an instructor, observer, or a supervisor, they show by action how they value pretend play and have faith in the learning it offers.

Working With Children to Further Their Play. When children are unfamiliar with play in a childcare or school setting with a large group of children and one or two adults, or if pretend play is not developing for whatever reason, there is a role that providers and teachers can take to teach children how it works. Providers and teachers help children understand how the ideas in their imagination can work alongside other children. Providers and teachers can guide children toward understanding the resources available to develop ideas in concert with others. The following recommendations for intervening to further play are drawn from the work of Sara Smilansky (1968, 1990). To help jump-start pretend play or intervene to support children in pretend play when there is a disagreement, childcare providers and teachers will want to keep in mind the following:

▶ Arrange for children to play in small groups of two, four, or possibly six children to keep the demands of what a child is juggling less complex while they experience the flow of pretending with someone else. Ms. Curtis was mindful of this as she watched Maria and Ruby play, and then Marco and Lawrence starting up their play right next to the two girls. She was mindful of the possibility that their pretend scenarios might collide so she stayed in close enough proximity so that she could see what unfolded. She was prepared to bring her calm voice and presence to bear on moments of tension as needed. She sees her role as stabilizing the situation long enough while the children talk through their problem.

▶ Read story books and act them out, particularly story books with animal characters. Stories such as *The Three Billy Goats Gruff* are a good way to encourage children to pretend to become a character other than themselves and practice the motions and words that a character (a good guy or a bad guy, an angry character or a scared one) might say. Acting out story books becomes a training ground for acting out the stories in their own imagination.

▶ Watch for moments when children may benefit from touching base with a provider or teacher. There are several elements in pretend play that may be reason to step closer to children or intervene to provide coaching to nurture emerging play skills. The elements of play that a provider or teacher watches for include:

– Children's use of objects to pretend such as a pencil being used to be the wand of a witch or a light saber for a space hero or a fire person's hose;

– Imitation of the actions and/or verbalizations of others in a prototypic role (mother, police person, doctor);

– Make believe regarding actions and a setting for the pretend story;

– Persistence in creating and sustaining play scenes;

– Establishing contact and connections with other children in the play scene;

– Connecting the play ideas of two children who are not playing at the moment;

– Sustaining interaction with others in a play episode;

– Participation in the negotiation and detailing of a play episode.

Childcare providers and teachers can intervene to nurture the growth of these elements in the following ways:

▶ Making suggestions: "How about you be the doctor and this is the sick child." Or saying to a child already engaged in play, "Help this mother with her sick baby? The baby is very sick."

▶ Making comments: "I see that your dog is hungry. He is eating a lot!"

▶ Asking questions: "What does the doctor say to the child's dad?"

▶ Demonstrating: "How about if we put the baby on this block and pretend it's his bed."

▶ Modeling: "Watch, I'll be the mother and I will feed the hungry dog a bone. 'Here doggie! Good Boy, you're eating your dinner!'"

Having located a child's current level of development on the rubric, providers and teachers then select one element of play at a time for focus when intervening. Providers and teachers use any one of the above comments with a child as free choice activity time evolves. The provider or teacher then watches the child's response to determine how effective it was in jump-starting the child's play to include the element being targeted. If the comment was helpful, that is, it furthered the child's play activity, the provider or teacher watches until the timing seems right to try another prompt. The child's response and receptivity are the gauge as to what is effective for a child at any one point in time. Depending on the child's age and temperament for pretend play, a child's play may develop slowly or more quickly. What matters is that children are given time and coaching in this activity that can be so valuable to finding friends and learning to get along in school subjects and routines.

Disputes in Pretend Play. When a disagreement or a fight erupts as will happen daily, providers and teachers will want to be close at hand to the children and listen carefully. There will inevitably be children shouting or crying, "Hey, that's mine! You took mine!" or "That's not how it works! You're supposed to…" The provider or teacher's first response needs to be moving in with a calm firm presence that immediately establishes safety for all and no blame – no judging the children as good or bad. The children are upset; the adult's job is to help untangle the conflicting points of view in the play scenario so that the children can renegotiate roles, the story line, and who is doing what.

Note: a key part of the benefits of pretend play in school and childcare is giving children time to make friends and learn how to grow inside of the ups and downs of a friendship. In pretend play, children have the chance to interact with and learn to get along with a wide variety of other children. As every provider and teacher knows, they cannot give a child a friend or force friendships to happen. What they can do is set the stage so that making friends is what is expected of everyone, that everyone in the group experiences respect, kindness, and full consideration of each other's needs. In such a setting, friendships among children are likely to unfold, and in the meantime, children learn to be friends with everyone.

What's important about play is that it can provide a lens for understanding the child on his/her own terms and how he or she manages with peers socially, emotionally, and intellectually. Pretend play provides a window for seeing the degree of creativity and spontaneity a child can bring to peer interactions as well as thinking in various subject areas.

Dictating and Acting Out a Story*

CHAPTER 7

- Significance of Dictating a Story and Acting It Out in Childcare and School

- Key Concepts and Skills

- Conducting the Assessment of a Child Dictating a Story

- Conducting the Assessment of Acting Out a Story

- Classroom Snapshot: Mrs. Martinez and Her Kindergarteners

- *Bridging* Assessment to Teaching

The activities of a child dictating a story and then acting it out with peers begin when a childcare provider or teacher invites a child to tell a story that she or he makes up while the adult writes down the words. Then, either in that moment or later the same day, the provider or teacher guides each child in acting out the story with peers. What's important is acting out the stories the same day they are written.

On a good day, children come into our classrooms or childcare excited to tell their teacher or provider as well as the other children about something they did, something they saw, or something they are anticipating with excitement. Children also want to play with friends to build with blocks, take care of their babies, go on an adventure using little figures of animals and toy cars, or draw pictures. Children have ideas and feelings that they long to find expression for. Their learning in school depends on their being open to taking in new experiences, and finding friends with whom they can share ideas and build new possibilities. The important part of these experiences is having the chance to put new ideas into words to someone who is listening. Learning to speak, and listen, as well as read and write are the most fundamental skills needed for schooling. That's what children dictating stories and acting them out provides: a curriculum in listening to words – spoken, written, and enacted.

---

*Adapted from Vivian Paley's teaching practices (1981, 1990, 2001).

Children dictating stories and acting them out has several parts:

1. Children compose a story that derives from the kinds of ideas they generate in pretend play or from their personal experiences. Stories often include familiar characters and plots from popular children's books, movies, or TV shows.

2. The teacher or provider serves as a scribe writing down the child's narrative which is usually a few sentences long or a paragraph at most.

3. While the teacher or provider is taking dictation, the child speaks and then listens, watches, and confirms the events and actions in the story that the teacher or provider is recording.

4. Later that day, the teacher or provider gathers children in a small or large group to act out stories that children dictated that day. Each story usually takes about two minutes to enact.

Significance of Dictating a Story and Acting It Out in Childcare and School

These two partner activities have powerful long-term benefits for young children as they begin learning what childcare settings and school are about and become apprentices in the processes of learning to read and write. Children's liveliness and willingness to come closer to stories and benefit from them emerge when they can pretend to be the story characters enacting imaginary scenes. Acting out the stories is where a major source of the learning comes for children. They gravitate and want to know more about every step in the processes of imagining, putting ideas into words, conveying them to the teacher or provider, and then seeing their ideas enacted with peers.

Dictating a story is an opportunity to cultivate children's oral language narrative skills while children also experience the affordances of the written word in recording their ideas. During dictation, children watch up close the transformation of their thinking from spoken word into print conventions. They also benefit from the experience of others, both providers and teachers and their peer group, being interested in their ideas. The classroom or childcare setting becomes a laboratory for expressing, listening, and revising story ideas.

As children act out each other's stories, they begin to see possible meanings vividly. This is where reading comprehension can begin. These listening, telling, and acting activities give children opportunities to hold multiple points of view in mind – those of the different story characters. This is what good readers and writers do. Story acting involves children in moving, interacting, discussing, and negotiating with each other to achieve a goal they are invested in – experiencing a story a peer has created.

Key Concepts and Skills

The **dictation** process makes it possible for each child to:

▶ Develop a concept of story:

– Visualize a scene in one's mind that is not present in the here and now and conveying it to others using words.

– Develop thinking and reasoning skills about problems and situations that are hypothetical and make-believe in a safe and reasoned way.

– Become aware of and use the elements and structure of different kinds of narratives, for example, fiction, nonfiction, a fable, and a fairy tale.

▶ Develop language skills:

– Expand language skills to verbalize and communicate ideas and feelings.

– Gain exposure to and familiarity with print conventions as each word is transcribed into letters and punctuation marks.

– Develop an interest in others' stories as a way to consider new possibilities for story plots.

Acting out stories, one's own as well as participating in acting out others' stories, affords children daily opportunities to:

▶ Examine story structure and word meanings closely as physical actions, gestures, and facial expressions along with words to make meanings visible.

▶ Gain a growing understanding of the logical necessity of one event happening before another and create a shared understanding of causal relationship among events.

▶ Develop social and interpersonal skills – learning to get along with a wide variety of people and their ideas; learning tolerance and consideration of others and their points of view; learning to negotiate while achieving a shared understanding of a situation.

▶ Learn to manage conflicts and one's emotional equilibrium through participation in the give-and-take process when developing and enacting story ideas.

Conducting the Assessment of a Child Dictating a Story

Materials. Story dictation requires paper and pencil only. When the provider or teacher asks, "What story do you have to tell?" they write down individual children's dictated stories on a piece of paper. It is a good idea to begin with 5″ × 7″ paper to keep stories brief and concise. Another possibility is each child having a spiral notebook where their dictated stories are recorded. This provides a record of a child's narratives over time.

Time. Dictation requires no more than two to four minutes per child. A provider or teacher spends time with an individual child taking dictation while the other children are engaged in activities in centers. Children need to know when to expect the opportunity to dictate stories and know the routines for indicating their wish to do so through a sign-up sheet or other system that the teacher or provider will create with the class.

Place. Dictation represents one medium available to children for the expression of their ideas. Providers and teachers can take dictation almost anywhere in the classroom or home care setting – in the block area, in an activity center. It can also be helpful to connect story dictation with a particular place, such as a writing and drawing table that is equipped with pencils, markers, erasers, scissors, rulers, crayons, and a variety of types of paper available to children to choose from when creating and composing a piece of writing, a drawing, or a mixed-media piece. The more resources available in an inviting and efficient way, the more likely children are to explore and use the materials in new ways. Providers and teachers will want to align story dictation with this location of resources for creative expression. Sitting at the story-writing table to take children's dictations can become the one reliable place children think of when they have a story to tell.

Another important aspect of this arrangement is that other children can readily sit at the table and listen in on a child's dictation, get ideas for their own stories, as well as offer ideas to the child dictating (who always has the choice of taking editorial suggestions or not). Teachers and providers will want to encourage this kind of listening, borrowing, and use of ideas among the children to create a literary community that benefits from and uses the ideas of others to try out a new story idea or point of view.

Scribe. Many teachers and providers feel that their time is too limited and stretched across many responsibilities to regularly take dictation. This is especially true considering how frequently children might request this interaction once they realize the satisfaction that can come from an adult attentively listening to their ideas. This is an area where teachers and providers can strengthen the activity by getting parent volunteers, other school staff, and even older children to come in on a regular basis to take down children's stories. Children benefit from regular opportunities to develop their ideas for a written story without having to focus on the mechanics of the actual writing while they juggle the details of a story plot.

Procedure. Teachers and providers play a critical role in arranging for story dictation opportunities in the classroom, and in using the opportunity to assess children. The work includes:

1. Select a time during the school day when you can be available to write down stories that children dictate individually. To initiate storytelling, the teacher or provider can watch the children at play and invite children to develop one of their play ideas into a dictated story that will be acted out.

2. Select a table where three to five children can gather to work on drawing, writing, or just listening and talking to others as dictation takes place.

3. Establish a routine where children take turns dictating stories, perhaps using a sign-up sheet or using the class roster and going down the list to give each child a chance to dictate.

4. Limit stories to writing on one side of a 5″ × 7″ sheet of paper (three to five sentences). Dictation will take approximately 1–5 minutes per child. As children grow more comfortable with more detail, you can expand the story paper to 8.5″ × 11″.

5. To begin the dictation process, sit with the child next to you on the side opposite the hand where you are holding the pencil. This way the child can see every mark you make on the paper and the correspondence between each spoken word and its transcription onto paper.

6. If the child needs a prompt to get started, ask, "How does your story begin?" or "What happens in your story?" Children may tell an original story or retell a familiar one.

7. During dictation, if a child pauses for five seconds or more, or says he or she is stuck, intervene with the following succession of prompts:

   a. Repeat the last sentence that the child dictated and then wait to see if that jump starts the child to continue.

   b. If the child needs additional prompting, ask, "What happens next?"

   c. If the child is possibly finished, ask, "Is there anything more in your story?"

   d. Reread the whole story and ask if there is anything else the child wants to add.

8. If a child demonstrates a motion or action to be included in the story, ask "How can you put that into words?" or "How shall I write that in your story?"

9. Sometimes a child has trouble finding words for their ideas and they might point or gesture with their hands or legs. You might try to offer words to express their desire. You can also invite other children nearby to listen and help offer words. Other children are hugely important to the success of these activities. You will want to rely on other children frequently. If a child says, "Ohhh put this into your story…" and offers an idea, you can support the idea of children offering each other help by asking the author, "Do you want that in your story? If you do, that's fine!" The storytelling and story acting activities are social activities, and the learning opportunities derive from their social nature. Children can benefit at every age from watching, listening, telling, and acting in each other's stories. They quickly learn to build on story ideas from books, nursery rhymes, and ideas that swirl around the room when good play and conversation are unfolding in their day.

10. When listening to a child dictate a story, providers and teachers will want to be mindful of writing down exactly what the child says, and not try to "clean up" or edit the child's language into proper grammar, particularly as they are getting started. It is important that the child hears themself and recognize each other's words as they would say them in pretend play. In time, you might ask the child who says, "Them went to the store." "Do you mean, *They* went to the store?" Whatever the child says, write it down even if it is grammatically incorrect. As the child hears him or herself, hears other children, hears you speak and tell stories, their words will adjust and absorb more conventional spoken forms. For children at young ages, and children who speak dialects of English, it is important that they first learn that what comes out of their mouth can be written down, and the process of dictation shows them this explicitly. In oral and written language development, the child moves from a focus on generating meaning, composing words to convey their thoughts, and then "cleaning up" or making more articulate their grammatical formulation of story ideas.

11. As the teacher or provider, you will want to be clear with children that all words we use in stories like all words used in our classrooms must be words of kindness and respect. Do not allow children to use words in play or in storytelling that hurt others in any way, or that are rude. The following example illustrates how this can be done. "Children, I will not write a story that has the words 'Shut up' in it because that is too rude. We do not say that to each other, and we will not have the characters in our stories say it either." Children respond immediately to these reminders and boundaries that keep them

safe in a respectful and kind setting. Storytelling is not permission to say anything we want. As teachers and providers who are role models, we ensure that these activities adapt to and reinforce the expectations and values of your home, childcare, or school. These activities become powerful and supportive of the children's learning to the extent that they are nested inside of and alongside the routines and practices you rely on to support and sustain the community values of safety, respect, and kindness.

12. As the child's dictation gets near to the end of the paper, tell him or her to think of a good ending as there is room for only one or two more sentences.

13. As the child finishes his/her story, ask if there is a title to this story. Also, ask the child as the author, which character he or she wants to be when the story is acted out.

Conducting the Assessment of Acting Out a Story

Now we turn to the second part of the story telling process: acting out the children's stories on the same day they were written. Acting out each child's story takes a few short minutes per story. It is not time consuming. That said, it is important to see the structure that holds the story-acting activity together, and the ground rules that keep it safe for everyone. The ground rules and procedures noted here come from observing hundreds of teachers and providers try out these activities and being able to now articulate what keeps the activities meaningful, safe, and fun for the children.

Materials.

▶ Children's dictated stories from earlier in the day.

▶ Open space for the group to gather to dramatize stories.

▶ A defined "stage" that could be a space marked out on the classroom floor with masking tape. It might also be a rug where children can sit along the four sides with the center of the rug denoting the stage.

Procedure. In the story acting activity, teachers and childcare providers become stage manager, acting coach, and role model for the children. They create a safe place for children to have ownership of the stories they compose and how they come to life. In getting started,

1. Have children sit in a circle around the edge of a rug or a class meeting area. Read and then act out one story at a time.

2. After reading a story, remind the author of the character he or she will play. Then the teacher or provider (not the author) asks one child after another sitting along the edge of the stage if they want to play the other characters in the story. If the child says "yes," the child comes onto the stage to join the actors. If a child does not want a particular role, the teacher makes nothing of it and asks the next child. Acting is a choice, not a requirement. The teacher or provider continues offering children a role until all characters have been assigned.

3. If the author of the story does not want to be an actor in his or her own story, use the procedure described above to assign all roles.

4. After roles have been assigned, read the story as written. The teacher or provider now becomes narrator and stage manager, directing and guiding the children's actions and signaling the beginning and end of each story.

5. The rules necessary to keeping dramatization safe and productive are:

    −   No touching anyone else ever. That is the most basic rule for safety and understanding: that everything is pretend.

    −   No leaving the designated stage area.

    −   No using any furniture or props. All story details are acted out in movement and gestures and facial expressions.

Dramatization takes about one to four minutes per story.

Rules. An important detail to keep in mind about the story telling and acting activities: they are structured rule-governed activities. The rules for story acting are the same as those that govern professional theater for a play such as "Lion King." In theater, everything is pretend. There is no touching. Once children understand this, everything is possible. They are experts at pretending! No leaving the stage: this is a good rule since children might get excited by a horse chasing a mouse and want to run around the room. A defined stage establishes the space where the pretending occurs.

The rules help children and the teacher or provider stay focused on the goal of the activity. The structure guiding the children's participation helps them get the most out of it. The goal of acting out a story is to listen to the words conveying a scene: the characters, their dilemma, and its resolution no matter how tiny a story is. When they are acting, children in effect, try on the circumstances to see how they feel, see what it is like to be the troll in *The 3 Billy Goats Gruff*, or the second little pig in *The Story of the Three Pigs*, and use language to portray their predicaments.

The guidelines for picking actors are set by the teacher or provider. The author picks the part he or she wants to play, and the teacher or provider guides the process for who plays the other characters. Vivian Paley found that when you let children pick the actors for their story, they pick their friends, and sometimes use the chance to exclude others whom they are upset with much as they might say, "You can't come to my birthday party." In order to ensure that no activity is a set-up for excluding others, or picking only one's friends, the teacher or provider handles that detail to keep the process fair and accessible to all.

There is plenty of room to improvise and try things in different ways while keeping the goals of acting in mind. For example, often with a story such as, "A bad guy and a horse," The teacher or provider can ask the author, "Can we pretend that everyone in the circle is a bad guy with a horse so we can act this out together?" Usually, a child will say yes. In this format, all children stand up, the teacher or provider invites the group to look like they are bad guys, and then invites them to pretend to have a horse on a lead. The teacher or provider might have the children pet the horse, pretend to get up on it, and ride it. This format gives everyone a chance to act out a character together.

Classroom Snapshot: Mrs. Martinez and Her Kindergarteners

In Chapter 2, we watch Mrs. Martinez introduce the children to storytelling and story acting by bringing two stories from children in last year's class to model what this new activity entails. Mrs. Martinez knows that over the next week, she will ask every child, "Do you have a story you want to tell that I can write down so we can act it out?" Today, she has introduced the possibility and there are children eager to get started.

Here is the story of five-year-old, Damian, who responded to Mrs. Martinez's invitation. Damian is eager and sure of himself as he dictates the following story.

Mrs. Martinez:	Tell me your story and I will write it down. How does your story begin?
Damian:	OK. The monster eat the boy. Then the little girl run to the boy's closet.
Mrs. Martinez:	Ok, wait now. Slow down. I want to get each word you are saying. The – monster – eat – the boy. Then – the little girl – ran... Where did she run to?
Damian:	The boy's closet.
Mrs. Martinez:	To – the – boy's closet. Ok. What happens next?

Damian watches Mrs. Martinez repeat each of his phrases as he dictates. He also watches closely as she echoes where she is in writing his words on the paper. Here is his finished story:

Damian:	There was a monster. There was a dog. There was Batman who was the dog's friend. Then the rabbit came and made Batman disappear and then the rabbit come and was Batman's friend. And they fight the bad guys. That's all!
Mrs. Martinez:	Good work. Let me read your story back to you.

She rereads his story and asks him, "Is there a title to your story?" He responds, "Batman and the Dog." Mrs. Martinez writes that at the top of his story paper.

Mrs. Martinez:	There's lots of action in this story. Who do you want to be when we act this out?
Damian:	Batman.
Mrs. Martinez:	OK. Let's see how many more actors we'll need. There's the little boy, the little girl, the monster, the dog, and the rabbit. And the bad guys. That's six characters along with you being Batman. That makes seven people plus bad guys. For the bad guys, can I invite anyone in the audience at the edge of the rug who wants to be a bad guy to play that part?
Damian:	Yeah!
Mrs. Martinez:	Oh, good. I know children will like that. You are all set. You can go back to your activity.

Damian runs back to the block area.

When it came time to act out the stories written that day, Mrs. Martinez guided the group to sit on the edge of the rug. She reminded the children to fold their legs so that the actors had room to play their parts on the stage, which was the area in the center of the rug.

Mrs. Martinez:	Boys and girls, Damian wrote a story that has his favorite character in it. Who's Damian's favorite character?! Who does he like to be when he is pretending?!

Children together, "Batman!!" [The children recognize that a day without Damian's Batman feels like someone missing from school.]

Mrs. Martinez:	Yes! Damian is going to be Batman. Damian, come on to the stage here. Now there are five more characters. Faith, do you want to be the monster?
Faith:	[She shakes her head "no."]
Mrs. Martinez:	OK, that's fine. Jordan, do you want to be the monster? [Jordan scrambles up fast to join Damian.]
Mrs. Martinez:	[pointing to Roberto] Do you want to be the little boy? [Roberto jumps up to stand on the rug in the circle.]

Mrs. Martinez continues offering the parts of the little girl, the rabbit, and the dog to each child who is next in the audience sitting on the edge of the circle. She does not worry about whether the part she is offering is a male or female character, and whether the next child is a boy or a girl. The character is just that − a person to pretend to be. A child can choose to play the part or decline it. The children learn quickly that parts in stories will come along daily, and plenty of them. They will grow at home with watching and acting − both being valuable ways to become absorbed in the story.

Mrs. Martinez continues: "Good, now we are ready for the acting. Remember our two rules when acting out a story: No touching anyone, and no leaving the stage. This is pretend. Let's see how this will work. Jordan and Roberto, the story starts with both of you. Come into the center of the rug here. Jordan, you're the monster. What does a monster look like? Show us what the monster looks like."

Mrs. Martinez continues to guide the children in their enacting of Damian's story. The energy and excitement are high. The challenge for the teacher or provider is to recognize that by harnessing their energy and excitement into the role playing of their character, she is bringing them closer to written language, its power, and its conventions − the basic skills at the root of their learning to read and write.

Interpreting assessment findings. As Mrs. Martinez reflected on Damian's effort to tell and act in his own story, she recorded his story as Level 3 in narrative structure. She saw that Damian brought together a set of characters that in the end fought the bad guys. The story was moving toward a Level 4 in that the characters could be developed to articulate further what brought them together. The story could also develop more of who the bad guys were and what they were doing.

Mrs. Martinez scored Damian's acting at a Level 4 on this first day of participating in the activity. Damian's working approach while dictating the story reflected strong initial engagement, focus, and goal orientation. Damian was eager for the action; he watched others as Mrs. Martinez organized the actors on the stage and he warmed up fast to acting. Damian also is not shy; he is comfortable offering ideas and is at home with being playful and imaginative. He brought these qualities to the story acting too. He could well move to Level 5 sooner than later. Damian could become one of those children who inspire and pull others along with him into expressive and dramatic performances of story scenes.

Bridging Assessment to Teaching

Story dictation and story acting contribute to the building of a literary community among children and teachers or providers. It is important for teachers and providers to remember that the rubric level of a child's narrative structure has no bearing on the deep pleasure, excitement, and interest children have in one another's stories. Children see and hear the seeds of good ideas in the making as they listen to each other whether the story is two or three words or paragraphs. The activities are inherently meaningful and powerful for young children. They pull children into speaking, telling stories, and becoming immersed in interactions with one another where they can grow in leaps and bounds.

Strengthening story dictation. An important dimension of inviting children into story dictation is to be mindful of the prompts used while taking down children's dictated stories. The rule of thumb in asking questions is to pitch the most open-ended questions first (such as, "Is there more?") and then follow up with more specific questions *if* the child can respond to the question with more developed ideas for the narrative. Teachers and providers sense when a question provides a springboard for the child to say more, and when a child is not ready to open up. With Damian, Mrs. Martinez saw no hesitancy in his certainty about his Batman story. Damian's story experience becomes a model for his classmates on how the activities work. Mrs. Martinez is off to a good start bringing the activities to this year's class.

Children sometimes copy phrases and words from story books into their own stories and this is a huge achievement. When children start their story with, "Once upon a time there was a girl," or "It was a sad day when the baby dinosaur got sick...," we get firsthand evidence that they are influenced by the flow of literary language in the stories being read to them. They are becoming attuned to the kinds of sentences and storybook phrases they can expect to hear when someone opens a book to read. The language of story books sounds different than when talking to friends. The language in books uses the same words we say when we speak but they flow in an up and down cadence that sounds very different when it is written down. Once children have heard written language, they will copy that too, just the way they do when they hear us say new words when speaking.

Teachers and providers can further children's development as storytellers in the following kinds of ways:

▶ Read stories often and from a wide variety of genres. With the opportunity for several read alouds during a full day childcare, preschool, or kindergarten, teachers and providers can be mindful of reading several different kinds of narratives daily that connect with different activities including fiction, informational texts (perhaps a biography or a science text about polar bears living in the artic), poems, fables, and song lyrics. Becoming at home with these various narrative forms provides children with an entree to becoming good readers and writers of all kinds of material.

▶ Help stories live in your classroom or home setting in as many different ways as possible: pretend play, creating puppets for puppet plays, having books on tape in a listening center, having a felt board with characters for telling stories or dictating them, and conversations during mealtimes.

▶ Have conversations with children during the day where they recount experiences from the past from a variety of situations and reflecting a variety of emotions. These conversations can be a place where they begin to recognize what will make good subjects to dictate or write about.

▶ Encourage children's pretend play. Help children make connections between the story ideas they play out with peers and the stories they dictate to be dramatized. Teachers and providers may spot a good story in the making during an activity time and might encourage a child who has not yet dictated a story to let you write it down for the group to act out later. Teachers and providers can prompt a child by saying, "Tell me your dinosaur story and I will write it down. I know the other children will love hearing it and we can act out what the dinosaurs are doing." Such comments demonstrate to children your interest in their stories.

▶ During and after stories have been dictated and acted out, teachers and providers can talk with the children as a group about the kinds of ideas that are emerging in their stories. Children are readily aware of characters and settings they like, the kinds of problems they encounter, and how they are solving them. Mrs. Martinez's children knew Damian and his story themes and characters readily. Teachers and providers can invite the children to reflect on what they notice about who likes to tell particular kinds of stories – for example, those who like animal adventure stories, those who like fairy tale themes, and those who like creating realistic family situations. This helps children notice both what they have been doing and other story forms that they might want to try out.

Strengthening story acting routines. Early childhood settings are a sea of movement. Acting out stories and role-playing solving problems are a logical and optimal way to make conscious ways of thinking and moving among participants in a group setting. Gesture and movement are universal means of communication and are ready media for young children to examine the logic and meaning of stories they dictate as well as those that teachers and providers read to them. Story acting is exactly what children learning a new language need: the chance to hear the story in words accompanied by simultaneous portrayal of the words in movement, gestures, and facial expressions.

Developing acting skills. The best way to cultivate skills in acting is to start with the tiniest of stories – nursery rhymes and finger plays. Many teachers and providers recognize the immediate benefit of finger plays and nursery rhymes using hand motions such as "Humpty Dumpty sat on a wall ..." during a transition point in the day. A collection of familiar and playful nursery rhymes can often provide the glue to having a good day with peers. They readily take children's minds off an unsettled situation and focus them in a physical and mental way on a story idea.

Another building block to dramatization skills is acting out simple adult-authored story books as a group, such as *The Three Billy Goats Gruff* or *Where the Wild Things Are*. One half of the group can be one character, such as the Billy Goats, and the other half of the group can be the other main character: the troll. By doing a group dramatization, children do not have to feel the initial self-consciousness that can come when acting alone in front of a group in a new setting. They can also watch others and compare their own actions to the possibilities repre-sented in the portrayal of a character's gesture or facial expression by other children.

Quick as a Cricket by Don and Audrey Wood is an ideal book to act out different animals, their movements, and dispositions. When guiding the acting out of such stories, teachers and providers can explicitly discuss and ask the children about the kinds of actions, gestures, and dialogue that support the meaning of the words in their mind, for example, "What does "slow as a snail" look like?

One detail that can be helpful when gathering to act out stories is to help children settle by singing a song or reciting a nursery rhyme using hand gestures. For example, a teacher or provider might recite "Jack be nimble Jack be quick, Jack jumped over the candle stick" as a sort of warm up acting activity – with the children and teacher or provider pretending to jump over a candlestick in front of them. The group is more prepared then for the acting of stories to come.

When dramatizing a story, poem, or song, teachers and providers can encourage children to imagine the feelings and ideas they are trying to convey to others. Questions such as the following can help:

▶ How can you show us that you are scared (or angry, surprised)?

▶ If you are an angry lion (or a puppy, or a powerful dinosaur), how can you let others know that? Show us what an angry lion looks like and what it does.

▶ How can you show that you are walking in quicksand (or swimming in the ocean, climbing into a spaceship)?

Finally, role-playing real-life dilemmas in the classroom can be a powerful way to integrate the need for problem-solving from stories to help children learn to get along well in real life. For example, if children are having trouble sharing blocks for building in the block area, a teacher or provider can create a simple story to be acted out by the children at group time. A teacher or provider might say that she has written a story and needs help to finish it.

After one group has role-played their idea, the teacher or provider can call four more children into the circle to stage their image of problem resolution. In this way, story acting can become an ongoing arena for exploring ideas right alongside the acting out of ideas from story books as well as the children's own stories, making the classroom experience a rich tapestry of written ideas that influence each other.

Once there was a group of animals who played in the forest: a lion, an elephant, a snake, and a duck. They wanted to build a house together. They found many great logs and tree branches to help them make walls for their house. As they began to build, they began to argue. Lion said, "Put that log over here." Elephant said, "No, I need it here!" Duck said, "No, it isn't supposed to look like that!" Snake said, "I have an idea. Give me all the sticks. I'll show you how to do it!"

The story is not finished. How are these friends going to build a house together? Show me one way you can imagine them building a house together." The teacher or provider then calls four children up to role-play this initial scenario and what might happen.

Storytelling and story acting are rich, exciting, and meaningful activities for children as young as two-years old right up through adulthood. As school-aged children grow more proficient in their own printing and writing, they can readily help take down dictated stories from younger children after they have experienced it with teachers or providers. This makes possible a wonderful apprenticeship for older children becoming good listeners and supportive friends and guides to younger children on the doorstep of learning to read and write, particularly in daycare settings.

Counting Collections*

CHAPTER #8

- Significance of the Counting Collections Activity in Childcare and School

- Key Concepts and Skills

- Conducting the Assessment

- Classroom Snapshot: Ms. Lamb and her Kindergarten Children

- *Bridging* Assessment to Teaching

The Counting Collections activity supports the development of an understanding of numbers and various counting strategies. Number knowledge extends beyond merely knowing number names and oral counting. The true essence of number knowledge lies in fostering children's number sense, which involves the ability to be flexible with numbers and understand relationships among them. Developing this deep knowledge of number sense builds the foundation that enables children to grasp concepts such as the decimal system, place value, and fractions with ease in later grades. As an assessment activity, Counting Collections in the *Bridging* assessment comprises three integral parts:

1. **Counting.** Children count the number of items in a collection of objects, such as craft sticks, marker tops, buttons, or bottle caps.

2. **Representing.** Children represent how many objects they count on paper using drawings, tally marks, and/or symbols.

---

*Counting Collections, with capital Cs, is based on research at the University of California at Los Angeles and the University of Washington. We borrowed many ideas from the book *Choral Counting and Counting Collections: Transforming the Prek-5 Math Classroom* by Megan Franke et al. (2018), as well as Erikson Institute's teacher professional development materials by Jeanine Brownell and Rebeca Itzkowich (personal communications, October 24, 2022; November 23, 2022).

3. **Conferencing.** The teacher engages in one-on-one conferences with individual children to discuss the strategies they used during counting.

Significance of the Counting Collections Activity in Childcare and School

Young children are constantly counting as they make sense of their world. Counting seems simple, yet it is quite complex. For example, the number of stairs children climb or the crackers they eat (cardinal number) is mathematically different from mom's cellphone number (nominal number), which is further different from the numbers on a clock (referential number). Counting and using numbers in these various ways is fundamental to learning mathematics in the early years of schooling and essential for human problem-solving. Children need time and opportunities across various settings to develop an understanding of counting principles and number relationships. Counting Collections supports this learning in the following ways:

▶ **Learn to count.** In Counting Collections, children count to find the total number of objects. While they count, children say number names in sequence, pair each object with one number name, and learn about the relationship between numbers and quantities. They gradually understand that the last number they uttered represents how many items are in the collection. Further, children learn that the rules or principles that govern counting apply to any collection. These skills are foundational in learning to count.

▶ **Learn ways to represent thinking.** Unique to Counting Collections is the invitation as well as the challenge for children to show how many they have counted. Over time with more experience and support from teachers, children learn different ways to represent counting results, such as drawing, graphing, writing, tally marks, and mathematical symbols. Representation serves as a sensemaking process for children and offers teachers insights into children's emerging mathematical thinking.

▶ **Learn counting strategies.** While carrying out this assessment activity, the teacher talks to each child about their representation to understand the strategies the child used to count the collection. For example, "How do you know for sure that this number [points to paper] and this number [points to collection] are the same?" "Can you show me how you got this number?" "I see you grouped the bears. Tell me how many are in each group." Over time and with repeated experiences, children identify and articulate their counting strategies. They also develop more advanced strategies that save time, making the counting process more efficient and accurate.

Key Concepts and Skills

Counting Collections supports the development of several key concepts and skills in mathematics, including:

▶ **Counting principles:** There are five separate and important dimensions to how numbers are used in counting. The five principles at work include:

1. *Stable order:* There is an ordered sequence of number names.

2. *One-to-one correspondence:* Each number corresponds to only one exact quantity.

3. *Cardinality:* The last number word in the count represents the total amount of objects in the collection.

4. *Order irrelevance:* Counting is not affected by the order of items counted in a collection.

5. *Abstraction:* The preceding principles can be applied to any collection of objects, whether tangible or not.

▶ **Counting strategies:** Different ways to count and organize items in a collection reveal varied problem-solving approaches and mathematical thinking strategies.

1. *Conceptual subitizing:* Learning to recognize "how many" without counting. For example, "I saw three fives, so 5, 10, 15."

2. *Counting on:* Starting with a given number and incrementing by one or more to find the next number in a sequence. For example, "Here are five buttons, so then there is 6, 7, 8…"

3. *Skip counting:* Counting by groups or in units, for example, by twos (2, 4, 6, 8…) or by fives (5, 10, 15, 20…) to quickly determine the total number of items. When skip counting, children use a new number word sequence or count units other than 1. They recognize a group of individual items such as 10 as a single unit, which allows children to work with larger quantities more efficiently.

4. *Number combinations:* Knowing basic combinations of numbers to develop mathematical fluency and problem-solving skills. For example, "10 plus 6 is 16; I know it."

▶ **Social learning:** Learning mathematics is a personal and social activity through which children develop confidence and proficiency in their mathematical skills. The social goals for Counting Collections include:

1. Children develop their **mathematical identity**, meaning they see themselves as comfortable and competent mathematics learners and problem-solvers in varied situations in and out of school.

2. Children learn to **discuss and converse** with others, such as counting partners and teachers, as they work through the task steps.

Conducting the Assessment

As we saw in Chapter 5 in Mrs. Martinez's kindergarten classroom, Counting Collections can readily be included during class choice time. Using regularly available materials in the classroom, the teacher works with two to four children for *Bridging* assessment.

Materials

▶ **Collections:** Bags of items that range in size and colors that are interesting for children to count and easy to collect, such as shells, rocks, craft sticks, markers, buttons, clothespins, counting bears, and playing cards. Such materials are found in dollar stores, classroom supplies, and garage sales. Name each bag for recording purposes based on the type of objects it contains, such as "Buttons" or "Seashells."

▶ **Counting quantities:** The size of the collection is tailored to the children's counting skills and offers built-in differentiation. An easy way to know the size range of the collections is to color-code them. For example, zip baggies with a pink slider are 10–20, zip baggies with a green zipper are 20–35, and so on. A good rule of thumb when offering children bags of items is to choose collections that stretch and challenge the child. This allows teachers and children to see what they are capable of. The upper ranges of counting sizes could be 10 items for 3–4-year-olds, 20 for 4–5-year-olds, and 30 for 5–6-year-olds (NCTM, 2006).

▶ **Organizing tools:** Offer children tools such as paper bowls, paper cups, egg cartons, ten-frames, and hundred charts when children are ready to make use of them.

▶ **Representational tools:** Clipboards with a recording sheet and pencil.

Procedures

▶ **Grouping.** Conduct the activity in small groups of no more than four children at a time. Each child works independently first and later possibly with a partner. This allows the teacher to conference with each child and note their mathematical thinking and strategies while working on the task.

▶ **Introduction.** The activity can be introduced in many ways as long as the teacher makes it clear that children need to do two things: (1) *counting* – count how many are in a collection of objects and (2) *recording* – show how many they counted and how they counted it. The introduction can be brief, but the teacher should be clear about the purpose of the activity – discovering how many. The teacher could invite children to help solve a problem by asking, "Can you help me figure out how many ____ are in the bag?"

▶ **Picking a bag of items.** Depending on children's counting abilities and experience, either hand a bag with quantities slightly challenging to the child's counting ability or let the child self-select a bag of objects to count.

▶ **Conferencing.** As children work on the task, the teacher will want to promote conversation about what items each child is counting, how many they are counting, how they can represent that quantity on paper, and how they figured out how many they have in all.

▶ **Documenting.** The teacher takes a photo of each child's counting materials, saves the child's recording sheet, and keeps notes on what each child says as part of the *Bridging* assessment documentation.

Classroom Snapshot: Ms. Lamb and Her Kindergarteners

Ms. Lamb has worked with her five-year-old kindergarten children on counting collections for a month since the beginning of the school year. In today's small group time, she gathered four children – Ayla, Tony, Mei-mei, and Sofia at a table for Counting Collections. As the children sat down around the table, Ms. Lamb gave each child a piece of paper and a bag. Each bag had different objects and quantities.

Ayla lined up all her rocks, a total of 10. Then she went back and touched each one as she counted. Ms. Lamb asked her how many, and she said "10" but wrote 5 on the recording sheet. She drew herself counting and drew each rock as she counted. When asked how many she drew again, she went back and counted each circle on the paper she drew.

Tony had a bag of nine toy cars, his favorite material. He quickly poured all the toy cars from the bag and started counting one by one.

Tony:	1, 2, 3, 4, 5, 7, 8, 9, and 10. I have 10 cars!
Ms. Lamb:	Can you count one more time?
Tony	1, 2, 3, 4, 5, 6, 7, 8, 9.
Ms. Lamb:	How many cars do you have?
Tony:	9

On the recording sheet, Tony drew three cars with wheels and then four squares. While drawing, he looked around to see what the other children at the table were doing and took a piece of rock from Ayla to put on one of his toy cars, "I am delivering!"

Meimei had a bag of 24 clothespins. She also lined them up but in three rows: ten on the first, ten on the second, and four on the third row. Interestingly, she spoke English for the first ten counting names and then switched to Cantonese for the rest of the counting.

Although she counted the clothespins correctly, Meimei looked confused about what the recording meant. She looked at Tony's drawing, started tracing clothespins one at a time, and left the table before completing the drawing.

Sofia's bag had a total of 10 marker caps. She lined them up in two lines, 5 on the top and 5 on the bottom, but counted them by twos: 2, 4, 6, 8, 10. Sofia then drew two lines of 5 circles and pointed to her drawing, "I have 10 marker caps."

Ms. Lamb watched closely as the children worked on their counting collections, noting what each child said and did while offering needed assistance. For Ms. Lamb, the children's responses illuminated the complexities in children's learning to count.

Conferencing With Students and Recording Assessment Findings. Ms. Lamb had a discussion with each child as they recorded their counting collections. She, however, focused on two children, Tony and Sofia, for her *Bridging* assessment today. Her conversation with these two children was as follows:

Ms. Lamb:	Tony, I noticed you drew some cars and squares. Can you tell me how many you have on the paper?
Tony:	1, 2, 3 4, four cars, 1, 2, 3, 4, four squares.
Ms. Lamb:	That's good; now how many are there altogether?
Tony:	1, 2, 3, 4, 5, 6, 7, 8, Eight together.
Ms. Lamb:	How do you know that the number of drawings on the paper is the same number of cars you just counted? Do you remember how many cars you have there?

Tony shook his head no.

| Ms. Lamb: | So, what can you do now to make sure they are the same? |

Ms. Lamb gave Tony a score of Level 3. Uses one-to-one Correspondence, based on the performance rubric. Specifically, Tony could use correct counting word sequence and one-to-one tagging strategy to count, but his cardinal number sense around 10 is fragile, and his recording is incorrect. Tony's scores for his productive working approaches were 4s for Initial Engagement, Focus and Attention, and Goal Orientation, as well as 3s for Planfulness and Resourcefulness. Ms. Lamb left the item for Cooperation empty because the activity did not offer this opportunity. For descriptive working approaches, Ms. Lamb gave Tony a 3 for Chattiness, Pace of Work, and Social Referencing, and a 4 for Playfulness.

The discussion with Sofia went as follows.

Ms. Lamb:	Tell me, Sofia, about your drawing here.
Sofia:	See, I have 5 marker caps here (pointing to the top line and tagging each circle), 1, 2, 3, 4, 5. I lined up 5 on the bottom, just like what I did on the top. 5 and 5 are 10.
Ms. Lamb:	That's interesting, so you don't have to count each one on the bottom to know there are also five there.
Sofia, proudly:	yeah, and I know 5 and 5 are 10.
Ms. Lamb:	When you were counting the marker caps, I heard you use a different way. Can you show me another way you can count these marker caps?
Sofia:	I can top and bottom, top and bottom, 2, 4, 6, 8, 10.
Ms. Lamb:	I am happy to know you can find many ways to count these marker caps.

On the Counting Collections Rubric, Ms. Lamb marked Sofia on Level 5, Count with Cardinality and Use Strategies. This means Sofia could count objects accurately up to 10, answer the "how many" of what question correctly, and use two strategies – skip counting and knowing a number combination. For the productive working approaches, Ms. Lamb gave Ayla 5 for Initial Engagement, Focus and Attention, Goal Orientation, and Planfulness. She didn't mark anything on Resourcefulness and Cooperation because of a lack of evidence. Throughout the activity, Ayla was relatively quiet, worked methodically, focused primarily on her own work, and appeared rather serious. She received 2s for all four descriptive working variables.

Bridging Assessment to Teaching

Counting Collections is a simple activity because it requires minimum preparation and instruction from the teacher on how to carry out the task, as well as little time for children to get familiar with the procedures. The activity is also powerful as it embodies a range of mathematical concepts and skills that children can practice extensively when this activity becomes an instructional routine in the classroom. Below are several ways that Ms. Lamb extends the Counting Collections assessment activity to various curriculum possibilities.

In addition to focusing on the assessment of two children, Ms. Lamb also noticed the need to work with her children on counting names and the stable order counting principle. For example, Tony skipped 6 in his first counting sequence. Ayla counted to 10 but wrote down 5. Meimei needed more time to acquire English words for larger numbers beyond 10. From this observation, Ms. Lamb thought about introducing more counting games and rhymes.

Inviting children to record their counting results on paper is relatively new to the class. Ms. Lamb realized that many children didn't quite understand what to do when asked to record how they counted, nor did they know the use of strategies to help count and record. From this observation, Ms. Lamb wondered if it was time for a class meeting to look at student work together. Perhaps she could ask Sofia to share her work and invite the children to discuss ways to organize the counting materials and consider different ways to count them.

Lastly, on both Tony and Sofia's rubrics for the productive working variables, there was a lack of evidence for resourcefulness and cooperation. Ms. Lamb knew that this was due to the activity goals she had in mind. At the beginning of the kindergarten year, Ms. Lamb believed it was appropriate to engage children in Counting Collections, a new activity, first individually. As children become more accustomed to the activity and have more skills in counting, she will invite children to work in pairs. The observational data Ms. Lamb collected on the four children give her a good sense of where each child is, how materials and language might affect children's work, and what opportunities she needs to bridge from assessment to teaching to further support her children's counting skills and mathematical understanding. As Ms. Lamb focused on task goals, the children, and her role as a teacher, she created a list of options she would pursue.

Task goals. When reflecting on children's experiences with the Counting Collections activity, Ms. Lamb thought about two areas of conceptual thinking involved and looked for ways to widen and deepen the children's thinking in both areas.

▶ *Counting skills:* To further the children's progress with counting, Ms. Lamb planned to enhance children's skills by:

  − Organizing the collections to include objects that capture children's interest;

- Being prepared to increase the number of items in the collections (e.g., 10 marker tops did not seem challenging enough for Ayla);

- Inviting and discussing different ways to organize and count larger collections (e.g., counting on, unitizing, skip counting);

- Looking at a larger collection with the group, estimating the number of objects, and then counting them to verify;

- Comparing one collection with another to estimate which one has more. When comparing a collection of dominoes and a collection of buttons in a jar of the same size, children will realize very quickly that the different attributes of the objects (size and shape, but not color) influence our perception of quantity; and

- Counting different tangible items as well as sounds, movements, and ideas.

▶ *Recording strategies:* Through small group discussions of three or four children, help children build a variety of ways to represent the collections accurately and efficiently they are counting, Ms. Lamb plans to ask questions such as,

- "How can you be sure you have 12 cars on the paper?"

- "If we had to put the cars away, would your paper show the same amount you counted?"

- "Is there another way to show me how many cars you counted?"

- "You have five lines of circles here [5, 5, 5, 5 + 2 circles on the paper]. Tell me why you are doing this?"

Children. When building bridges between assessment findings and follow-up teaching activities, Ms. Lamb reminded herself of the following starting points about children.

▶ *Every child counts.* Regardless of family background and parent education level, whether in rural or urban settings, under-resourced or affluent communities, English or non-English speaking, everyone counts and has countable materials at home. One of the first mathematical activities that parents engage in with their children is counting. It is a teacher's responsibility to be alert and aware of information about what kinds of materials young children encounter at home and how counting emerges at home so that school activities can build on this base of familiarity and experience.

▶ *Multilingual learners.* Encourage children to express their counting in their home language alongside English to allow them to build a bridge between their existing numerical understanding and English numeracy. Promote partnerships between English-speaking children and English language learners, encouraging them to count together and share their numerical knowledge. This fosters language exchange and peer learning.

▶ *Agency.* Let children decide how to organize their collections and whether they want to use plates or cups or other tools such as ten-frames or hundred charts to help them organize their counting. When children play with collections of materials, discover new ways of counting, and talk about their efforts in group discussions, their confidence and sense of agency grow along with their proficiency in the different aspects of number concepts.

▶ *Counting partners.* Children can work alone, but the advantage of schooling is the chance to learn from others. When children work in pairs, we recommend that children count with partners at a similar developmental level. In the process, they learn to consider their peer's perspectives on the problem and how to approach it. In addition, the process of counting and recording the count engages the partners in negotiation and problem-solving. In these interactions, the focus is on children's effort to express their thinking and try to come to an understanding of someone else's view of the problem.

▶ *Time and effort.* Mathematics is similar to a participatory sport. Children need ample experience with the same task over weeks and months to become more skillful.

Teacher. Ms. Lamb also reflected on how she could build a sense of challenge into the Counting Collections activity while not moving too fast for the children. For Ms. Lamb, it is important to remember that the development of number concepts takes months and years, not days or weeks, to unfold. While development is happening, children need the careful ear and eye of an attentive teacher to tweak and support their efforts in thinking.

▶ *Instructional routine*

  – Implement the activity regularly in the classroom as an ongoing instructional routine. Featuring the activity once or twice a week makes a difference if it occurs year-round.

  – Change the number of items in each collection bag frequently. This addresses the problem of children arriving at the number of objects in a bag as if it were a fixed amount, assuming the total and announcing it to other children.

- Work with colleagues to arrange opportunities to count with children in another classroom of the same age or a bit older or young children in the school.

- Be mindful of children developing a sense of their own identity as someone who is good at mathematics, can think mathematically, and likes seeking patterns and relationships among variables in a problem to be solved. Develop children's mathematical identity by using their ideas as the launch pad for more sophisticated mathematical concepts and skills.

- Keep the activity open-ended and child-centered by encouraging children to discuss what they are doing and drawing with their partner(s).

▶ *Observations, conversations, and reflections*

- Walk around to watch and listen to children while they are working on their counting collections and ask a question or challenge children's mathematical thinking and extend their understanding.

- Confer with children about their conception of quantities and ask children, for example, whether they can count the same collection in a new way, whether they can count by 2s, 5s, or 10s, and whether they can use some tools to make the counting easier.

- Engage in reflection with the whole class periodically to highlight children's varied strategies to help spread new ideas among the children and provide new counting challenges for children to anticipate.

▶ *Connection to other classroom activities*

- Counting within the context of various classroom routines, such as determining the number of cups needed for lunch or the number of pencils needed for everyone in the class to have one for drawing a picture.

- Read children's counting books like *Quack and Count* by Keith Baker and *Mouse Count* by Ellen Stoll Walsh. Lead the group in reciting counting nursery rhymes, such as "One two buckle my shoe...". Play finger games that include counting, such as "Five, Green, and Speckled Frogs..." and draw children's attention to experiences the class is having with Counting Collections.

- Involve counting in playful activities in the block area by asking children, which tower is higher and why. During dramatic play, you might invite children to count money and price the goods in the grocery store, for example.

Drawing a Self-Portrait*

CHAPTER
#9

- Significance of Drawing a Self-Portrait in Childcare and School

- Key Concepts and Skills

- Conducting the Assessment

- Classroom Snapshot: Ms. Cotter and Her Children in Childcare

- *Bridging* Assessment to Teaching

How children depict themselves in a setting using pencil and paper reveals a great deal about hand-eye coordination, experience with the tools for drawing (and writing), and conventions used to represent people and objects around us in two dimensions. Every aspect of drawing has to be learned: how to hold a pencil, approach a piece of paper as a space for creating a visual image, envision details that can be portrayed, make decisions to transform a mental image into lines on a piece of paper that depict the scene, and finally being able to explain to others the meaning of the lines. Drawing a self-portrait offers many opportunities to gather information about children's thinking, drawing skills, and feelings about themselves with others.

For this activity, children are invited to draw a picture of themselves either at home, in childcare, or in school. They are given an 8.5 × 11″ sheet of white paper with a #2 pencil along with a small hand-held mirror. If providers and teachers have access to skin-tone colored pencils, they are ideal. The children's task is to create a picture of themselves with details that show where they are and who they are with. That's all!

Significance of Drawing a Self-Portrait in Childcare and School

Throughout human history, people (both adults and children) have developed three ways to represent and communicate ideas and feelings to

---

*The work in this chapter builds heavily from the work of Nancy Smith in *Art and Experience* (1993).

one another: through gestures and bodily movements (enactive mode of representation); visually with drawings, paintings, and photos (iconic mode); and symbolically through language encompassing spoken, signed, and written forms (Bruner, 1966). Proficiency in creating and interpreting visual representations is a crucial aspect of human development and is shaped by social and cultural influences. Schooling depends on understanding and learning to express ideas both verbally and visually, as well as understanding a wide range of graphic illustrations in various books and documents. Therefore, learning to draw is not just a skill for the arts; it directly impacts learning to represent ideas across a wide range of disciplines in the long run – the sciences, mathematics, the humanities, as well as the visual arts. The self-portrait activity supports young children's development in the following ways:

▶ **Expressing Ideas Visually:** The self-portrait activity provides experience in the iconic mode of representation, allowing young children to practice their drawing skills. The activity encourages children to use the elements of lines and shapes to create something meaningful, and in doing so, fostering their creativity and imaginative skills.

▶ **Promoting Self-Identity:** Creating a self-portrait encourages children to explore and recognize their own unique physical characteristics in a setting where a variety of different children are doing so too. This activity can help promote a sense of self-awareness and self-identity as they study their own image and learn to appreciate their own and other's individual features.

▶ **Understanding Diversity:** The act of creating a self-portrait is not only personal but also social. When children look at the portraits of their classmates, even if it is only using pencil, they can vividly see the differences among their peers in terms of gender, the shape of the eyes, or the way their hair grows and frames their face. This provides children with the experience and concrete understanding of the concept of diversity.

▶ **Practicing Brain-Hand-Eye Coordination:** Drawing requires coordination and control of hand movements in sync with an unfolding mental image and an eye toward what goes on the paper and where. As children learn to manipulate a pencil, they improve their hand-eye coordination and dexterity as they convey details in facial features and body proportions using lines, shapes, and positioning of them on paper.

▶ **Furthering Observational Skills:** Through this activity, children are encouraged to attentively observe themselves in their immediate surroundings. They begin to notice details about their own facial features, hair, clothing, and the space they occupy. They also become aware of their peers alongside them doing the same.

This heightened attention to detail not only contributes to children's artistic development but also enhances their broader observational skills, drawing experience, and social awareness.

▌ **Fostering Cognitive Development:** Drawing a self-portrait encourages spatial reasoning, representational skills, and problem-solving. Children must analyze shapes and proportions and make decisions about how to represent themselves in a place with others on paper, all of which promotes cognitive growth.

▌ **Supporting Language Development:** The discussions in every aspect of this activity are critical to the learning that is possible for children in this activity. The more children have a vocabulary for talking about their individual characteristics and how to represent them in drawing, the more awareness they bring to observing and developing their skills making lines and shapes to communicate meaning. Discussing their self-portrait with peers provides an important opportunity to cultivate skills in communicating more clearly and with respect.

Key Concepts and Skills

When children draw, they are thinking; they are working on conveying an idea. Experiences in the visual arts, and with drawing in particular, develop children's control of tools, their familiarity with materials, and their discovery of techniques that contribute to creating and communicating meaning. The seminal work of Nancy Smith set out the key concepts young children are learning when they draw:

▌ **Tools:** When engaging in creating a drawing, children inevitably first examine and explore the properties of the tools and materials they will work with in this two-dimensional activity. Children explore the properties of materials (for example, how hard to press the pencil, how to make a fat or thin line) and their creative potential for representing and communicating ideas and feelings.

▌ **Surface:** Children learn about the possibilities and constraints of a two-dimensional surface, the paper in this activity – its edges, borders, the features of the surface – how smooth or textured it is and how that affects the lines one draws on it.

▌ **Lines, shapes, and the motions that make them:** Children gradually gain control of hand and finger movements while holding a pencil to explore mark-making and the shapes and forms that can be made on paper.

▌ **Pattern and composition:** With experience, children begin to recognize shapes that are pleasing, and experiment with repetition and arrangements of them on paper in ways that capture and communicate an idea.

▶ **Conventions:** The more children draw, the more awareness they gain of conventions to represent meaning, features of a human figure, or common objects found in one's environment, while learning to recognize visual conventions others use in books and in one's community to communicate information and feelings.

▶ **Developing an eye for detail:** With guidance and encouragement, children will look closely at an object, or thinking about an idea to explore ways to represent its meaning in a form that captures the quality and feeling of an experience in a 2D representation.

▶ **Developing discussion skills:** When children come together in a small or large group, discussing the features in their own work, and wondering what other artists do in their drawings, becomes possible. Childcare providers, teachers, and children can learn from one another when regular opportunities are provided to explain and discuss choices made and details in drawings that depict ideas one wants to convey.

Conducting the Assessment

Set up and materials. Drawing a picture of oneself in a familiar setting, at home, childcare center, or in school, is one way providers and teachers invite children to introduce themselves to the group. The finished pictures offer a way to create a representation of the class as a group and as a community. Allowing children to pick the setting where they portray themselves offers a measure of choice for children to think about themselves where they are comfortable. Drawing a self-portrait is done with pencil and paper only. The choice of pencil alone for this task is intentional. The goal is to observe the child's drawing skills. Using a #2 pencil, the child focuses on making lines, shapes, and shading rather than color. In addition, the child is less likely to be distracted by the imprecision that can result when using tools such as crayons or paints. If teachers and providers have access to skin-tone colored pencils, these can be ideal for this activity making it possible to discuss and represent racial colors of skin, eyes, and hair while still focusing on lines and shapes.

In planning to carry out the activity, childcare providers and teachers will want to invite a small group of children at a time to a table to create their self-portrait. This makes it possible for children to be with others whom they can talk to and compare notes with as they go. It allows the provider or teacher to observe both what they do while drawing as well as how they approach the activity. Keeping the group small makes careful listening and observation of the dynamics possible.

Procedure: For this activity, providers and teachers give children a piece of unlined 8.5″ by 11″ white paper plus lead pencils; they can be thin or thick pencils. If possible, use skin-tone colored pencils. Also, the children will want access to a small hand-held mirror to be able to look at their faces for details such as their eyes, hairline, where their ears are, and the shape of their nose.

1. Give children pencils and paper. Ask them to: "draw yourself at home or in childcare, or in school." Emphasize the need to show others where they are in their home or childcare, or classroom, and what the room or area looks like.

2. Encourage children to use a mirror to check features on their face that they might want to include in their drawing.

3. Invite children to work as long as they can on their drawing, adding further details as they go along, and perhaps talking to others around them about what is in their drawing.

4. When a child is finished, ask the child to describe details in the picture for you. This will provide an opportunity for the provider, teacher, and other children nearby to hear the child's thinking about the meaning of certain lines or shapes that are not immediately evident. If the child describes details that cannot be seen in the picture, this opens an opportunity to invite the child to add the details to the picture she or he is describing. For example, if a child says her grandmother is happy to have snack with her after school, the provider or teacher might ask the child how she could show the grandmother looking happy, and show them eating, to see if the child adds anything to the picture.

Classroom Snapshot: Ms. Cotter and Her Children in Childcare

Ms. Cotter has a small group of children aged three to six in her childcare program. She has had daily discussions with the children about their families and making friends. She has made use of Margaret Wise Brown's picture book, *The Important Book*, in several ways. Each page portrays a simple object in daily life such as the grass, the sky, an apple, and the shoes we wear daily with two or three sentences about what makes each one important. Ms. Cotter has built on this poetic noticing of what is around us all to introduce classroom materials one by one to the group so that the children notice every detail of the object, how it is used, where it will be kept in the classroom, and what's important about it. The last page of M. W. Brown's book talks about what makes each individual child important. Ms. Cotter extends the conversation initiated by this book to invite the children to discuss what is important about themselves.

Ms. Cotter tells the group that they will draw a self-portrait, a picture of themselves at home or in childcare that will be displayed on their bulletin board. She asks the children to come to the drawing-writing table to create their self-portrait. She is eager to watch how each of them sits in a chair, holds their pencil, and begins the task of depicting themselves in a setting.

The children settle in around the table. Ms. Cotter brings a basket with small hand-held mirrors along with #2 pencils. She passes each child a piece of white paper and invites them to think about whether they want to draw a picture of themselves at home or in childcare. She tells them, "I've gathered mirrors here in case you want to look at your face to check details about your eyes or nose that you will want to include in your picture." The children pick up a pencil and begin to draw.

The drawings of two children were particularly striking. One five-year-old boy, Jason, immediately began what became an elaborate drawing that quickly took on qualities of a cinematic rendition of his favorite fantasies of action figures in a spaceship drama. His drawing was an extension of the dramatic play he engages in any chance he gets. Ms. Cotter learned quickly that his huge appetite for action figure dramas could be transformed onto paper. Jason held the pencil adeptly and it seemed to keep pace with the image he held in his mind's eye. He first drew four figures each with hair, eyes, big smiles, a shirt, and feet. Each guy was on a skateboard with the palms of their hands opened out shooting webs as Spiderman does. They each had big smiles, and one was wearing glasses (Jason wears glasses). One of the four had a small string of hearts coming from his hands and encircling his head. Another had a thinking bubble above his head in the shape of a huge heart. Jason said that the guy was happy (there were no words in the bubble). Overhead, there were two airplanes, a hot air balloon, and eight big fluffy clouds. Jason's fully animated drawing reflected him at home and in childcare. Ms. Cotter recognized that this was Jason at his happiest – in his imagination! Jason kept a running monologue going as he was drawing telling the story of "the guys" on an outing. His drawing reminded Ms. Cotter of a modern-day Robin Hood story.

Six-year-old Marissa's drawing offered a striking contrast. Ms. Cotter described her as one of the shy quiet children in the group. The major part of her drawing was a picture of her home: a tall apartment building five stories tall with a traditional house rooftop. Each floor of the building had a carefully drawn staircase to the next floor and a window with panes marking the glass. On the top floor of the building, the fifth story, there was a tiny figure of a girl sitting on a chair that looked like the letter "h." Marissa also drew a girl at the door to the building at the foot of the first stairway. Both figures of herself showed a girl with long pigtails, a big smile, hands reaching out, and a happy demeanor. Marissa said that the girl at the front door was her coming home from school, and the girl upstairs was her doing her homework. The only time she talked was when Ms. Cotter asked her to tell her about her picture.

Ms. Cotter scored Marissa's picture at a Level 4 and Jason's at Level 5 on the performance rubric. Ms. Cotter acknowledged that the two children could not be more different in personality and in their working approaches as well as in the content of their drawing. Jason was outgoing and talkative with the other children as he drew, whereas Marissa was as quiet as a mouse. Both children received scores of "4" on the first three productive working approaches: Focus of Attention, Goal Orientation, and Planfulness. Regarding Resourcefulness and Cooperation, these two variables were not relevant as neither child hesitated or got "stuck," and neither child was called upon to help someone else or saw a need to do so. With no evidence for either of these two variables, Ms. Cotter left them blank. For Descriptive working approaches, the two children both scored a 3 on Pace of work and a 1 on Social referencing. Neither child checked in with others while working as they had their own idea for what they wanted to draw right from the start. The two children were the opposite though when it came to Chattiness and Playfulness. Jason was talkative in narrating the antics of the four characters out on skateboards, and Marissa never said a word.

Bridging Assessment to Teaching

The self-portrait task offers childcare providers and teachers with the opportunity to imagine the context that will give rise to the children's best effort: the time, space, materials, and mindset for approaching drawing. Essential elements of the setting for this task include the following, many of which Ms. Cotter had in place:

- Provide multiple opportunities for unstructured drawing with pencil and paper during the day. This can be encouraged by allowing children to make use of resources at a drawing/writing table or center stocked with the various tools that visual artists and writers might want to draw on.

- In different curricular areas, have children draw common objects relevant to the lesson they are working on. If there is a discussion of fish in a nearby pond, or a tree, providers and teachers can use children's drawings to compare/contrast the different ways children are using line and shape to represent the same object.

- Welcome opportunities to talk with children about their drawings.

- Have children draw a real object, and contrast this with drawing an object from memory. Compare and contrast the products of both processes. Providing the children with mirrors as they create a self-portrait is an example of how children might move back and forth between what they see in the mirror and what they imagine as they portray themselves on paper as Ms. Cotter did.

- Use reproductions of drawings from different artists and different cultures to support children's awareness of how line, shape, and composition can be used to represent objects and people.

- Examine drawings of the human figure in the many illustrations in children's storybooks and discuss how details are represented by different artists using different techniques to create different feelings about the characters.

Using a pencil to draw a visual image of an object is a learned skill. Frequently young children will say, "I can't draw a house [or an animal, or person]. Will you do it for me?" It is important that providers and teachers convey to young children that drawing skills are learned. As with all skills that we learn, it is important that the environment values drawing, provides a place to get materials readily, and provides frequent opportunities to observe, draw, and discuss drawings – one's own and those of others. In such a setting, it is not necessary for a provider or teacher to draw for a child, although inviting other children to draw their version of an object and talk about how they do it can be a great way to open conversations about how to get started.

Comments and questions while watching children drawing: The important detail in seeking to assess children's drawing skills is the need to observe them while they are working on a drawing. That is where the clues are as to what they are working on and where providers and teachers can uncover the meaning of the child's marks on paper. When observing a child with a pencil in hand, a provider or teacher can tell whether it is the paper and the pencil itself that absorbs the child's interests, the surface of the paper, the movement of the pencil, or the substance of the figure being drawn. Different kinds of questions that providers and teachers might ask themselves given what one notices include:

▶ What does the child's effort suggest about his or her level of experience with using pencils for drawing?

▶ Is the child's primary focus on the physical act of making marks on paper, or is the child also focused on making a representation?

▶ What does the child's words and actions while drawing suggest to you about their focus? What can the child tell you about his or her drawing?

▶ What does the child spend a good bit of time on while drawing?

When wondering about children's intentions, Nancy Smith offers guidelines for the kinds of questions providers and teachers will want to ask children that derive from knowing the developmental rubric levels. The starting point for childcare providers and teachers is observing and listening to children while they draw and being responsive to what they say and do. When the child is nearing completion or is done, providers and teachers will want to carefully put words to what they see to offer a starting point for the child to talk about their drawing. The following chart summarizes features of several stages of development that Nancy Smith identifies and the kinds of comments from a provider or teacher that can be helpful at that stage (Table 9.1).

Table 9.1 Children's Development in Painting With Adaptations for Drawing

STAGES	WHAT CHILDREN ARE THINKING ABOUT, WORKING ON, AND DISCOVERING AS THEY ENGAGE WITH MATERIALS	COMMENTS AND QUESTIONS THAT ARE HELPFUL TO CHILDREN IN THIS STAGE WHILE THEY ARE INVOLVED WITH MATERIALS
Motions and the Marks They Make	• Child's focus is on the kinesthetic, sensory, bodily movements that accompany putting marks on paper. They are not involved in representing anything in particular but rather are exploring arm and hand movements and what they make.	• Observe – watch closely what children do with the pencil. • Listen to what children say. • Describe what you see children do with materials. This helps give them a vocabulary for the tools they are using and the effects they make. • Enjoy children's work! Display some of it.
Finding Out About Lines, Shapes, and Colors	• As visual-motor coordination increases, children explore making lines of different lengths, experimenting where they put them on paper, and varying the directions in which they move across the paper. They experiment making patterns with repetition and variation of lines, shapes, and colors. They explore these visual-graphic elements to produce specific and varied results.	• Describe for the child what you notice about lines and shapes he or she has made. • Offer children choices as to what pencils and types of paper they want to work with. Articulating options helps children become conscious of noticing differences. • Help give children words to discuss their work: the kinds of lines (straight, curved, wiggly), color tones (light, dark), nature of shapes (round, bumpy, rectangular), location of shapes and lines (top, center, bottom, or side of paper).
Making Designs	• Having mastered the basic concept of paper as a continuous surface space	• Listen carefully. • Describe what you see noticing where the child

(Continued)

Table 9.1   (Continued)

STAGES	WHAT CHILDREN ARE THINKING ABOUT, WORKING ON, AND DISCOVERING AS THEY ENGAGE WITH MATERIALS	COMMENTS AND QUESTIONS THAT ARE HELPFUL TO CHILDREN IN THIS STAGE WHILE THEY ARE INVOLVED WITH MATERIALS
	with top, bottom, side, center, and edges, children create pages of patterns and designs using distinct colors and forms that create an organized whole.	puts colors, shapes, and lines.
First Representations	• Children begin to find and name objects in their drawings and paintings – family members, pets, roads, airplanes, crashing or exploding objects, a TV character doing something and even letters of the alphabet or numbers.	• Listen first. The child will name representations when that is his/her intention. Encourage children in open-ended ways to talk about his/her picture: "Tell me about your painting. What have you been working on?" • Let the child do the naming and labeling.
Simple Images: People, Houses, and Animals	• Children begin to organize, focus, and narrow down their topics for paintings and drawings. Children use symbols for people and objects, the attributes for which become more differentiated in time with experience. The first symbol for people emerges, what has been called "the universal tadpole" – a circle with lines coming off it to represent arms and legs. Children create a setting for their images and are conscious of depicting real and imaginary worlds.	• Listen. • Be responsive to the thinking of the child. • Describe what you see. Notice details, themes in the child's work, what you notice over time. • Enjoy, appreciate, and open possibilities for the child to keep exploring.

Source: Adapted from Smith et al. (1993).

Furthering Children's Drawing Skills: The following guidelines offer ways that childcare providers or classroom teachers can further children's drawing development.

▶ The library area will want to offer many opportunities to examine the work of illustrators – different ways artists have devised to give expression to ideas in a visual format in addition to the verbal. For example, providers and teachers might have children look closely at the line drawings of children and families in Ruth Krauss' book, *A Hole is to Dig*, and then notice the drawings of family members by Ezra Jack Keats' in his books about Peter such as in *Peter's Chair*. There are the colorful collage figures of people and animals in both Eric Carle's books and those of Leo Lionni. Providers and teachers will want to include books in the library collection that represent a range of visual media. Discussing the style and techniques an author and illustrator use draws attention to the decisions writers and illustrators make about what can best be conveyed in words, what details are better conveyed with a drawing, and how words and drawings can complement each other.

▶ Have a group of children use pencils to draw the same object from different points of view (perhaps a tree, or building, or an object in the classroom that the class is interested in (perhaps a class pet, or a favorite plant). Compare and contrast how the same object is represented from different perspectives.

▶ Encourage children to use different media (pencil, paint, crayon) to represent the same subject. Display these works and discuss how different materials influence the way objects are represented.

▶ At different points in time, have children use pencils to draw the same object or experience. Compare the drawings, calling attention to similarities and differences in how they represent the same subject. Pay particular attention to the use of different techniques. This is where drawing self-portraits at different times in the school year can be both fun and informative for the child and others to see their change over time. In one early childhood program, we observed the self-portraits from a class of three- and four-year-olds done in September, January, March, and then in June at the end of the school year. The children and their families loved looking at the drawings and what new details showed up each time they did a new portrait.

Strong House for the Three Pigs

CHAPTER

#10

- • Significance of the Strong House for the Three Pigs in Childcare and School

- • Key Concepts and Skills

- • Conducting the Assessment

- • Classroom Snapshot: Ms. Imani's and Her Preschool Children

- • *Bridging* Assessment to Teaching

There is a good reason that the story of *The Three Little Pigs* is such a favorite: as children get big enough to leave for school, they are aware of all the ways that the familiar, safe world they are used to might be blown away. When this *Bridging* activity invites them to build a "strong" house, it gives children a way to think about the different ways to be "strong" at the same time as it introduces them to science, technology, engineering, and mathematics (STEM) concepts and ways of thinking.

▶ Children's experiences in this activity are guided in using the scientific method to test a hypothesis – a possible idea, about how to construct a house and consider improvements;

▶ They learn about technology as they explore materials and tools for making a strong house;

▶ They participate in the engineering design process as they move from defining the problems involved in making a strong house to trying out a solution using the materials at hand and working with each other to consider different structural possibilities; and

▶ They are using mathematics as they figure out the size, shape, and dimensions for materials they need.

The activity is designed to be carried out over several days or even weeks so that children have plenty of time to explore and make discoveries about the many ways a house – or anything else – can be strong. For this activity in particular, it is important that childcare providers and teachers move slowly giving children plenty of time for each step in the process to explore, think, try out ideas, and discuss what they are finding with peers and their teacher or provider. The process of carrying out the activity is where the rich learning resides. The activity has several parts:

1. The teacher or childcare provider begins by reading a simple version of the traditional fairy tale, "The Three Little Pigs," several times to children over a week. After each reading, the teacher involves the children in acting out the story followed by an open-ended discussion about the characters, setting, sequence of events, and the dilemma faced by the pigs.

2. The teacher guides small groups of children in building houses for the pigs using the materials provided. Children then put their designs to the test by subjecting them to the forceful blowing of the wolf.

3. Children participate in large group discussions of what worked and what didn't work in building strong houses after putting their houses to the test of huffing and puffing. The children then collaborate to build newly designed strong houses.

Significance of the Strong House for the Three Pigs in Childcare and School

The Strong House for the Three Pigs is a dynamic STEM activity designed to engage children in multifaceted learning experiences. This activity incorporates the following key elements:

▶ **Focus on essential questions:** Essential questions "get to the heart of the matter" in children's learning. The Strong House activity invites children's curiosity by addressing essential questions relevant to STEM learning, such as "What will make this house strong?" and "How can we make sure the house is strong using the materials we each have?"

▶ **Contextualize STEM learning:** Using a beloved children's storybook as the starting point for an activity is widely recognized as an effective approach to interdisciplinary learning with children. By immersing children in an engaging story, the Strong House activity readily establishes a problem that the children can identify with and want to work on together. As children work to protect the pigs in a safe home, they are also engaging in the engineering design process, conducting scientific experiments to inform their designs, applying mathematical concepts to address challenges, experimenting with various technologies, and communicating their thoughts verbally or through drawing, writing, and creating models.

▶ **Engage in the engineering design process:** At the core of the Strong House activity lies the engineering design process, which guides children in small and manageable steps in identifying goals and challenges, imagining possibilities, making plans, creating structures, and working to improve them when they fall over. When children work alongside each other watching and discussing houses that keep falling down, they learn that setbacks and even failure are an integral part of coming up with a successful design. As teachers and providers guide children in collaborating and thinking more deeply about problems, children are experiencing the essence of good schooling – learning alongside supportive friends.

Key Concepts and Skills

Strong House for the Three Pigs supports the development of several cross-cutting concepts in STEM, including:

▶ **Properties of materials:** Materials have unique qualities. Clay is squishy and moldable, while craft sticks are sturdy and can hold things together. These properties dictate whether a material is right for the job. For instance, the stiffness of index cards works better than paper for building a strong house. Children build a structure in this activity while considering the affordances of different materials like clay, craft sticks, and masking tape.

▶ **Structure and function:** How things are put together affects how they look, stay steady, and how well they work. Engineers think about materials, shapes, and how to arrange different parts to make things strong and functional. As children think about a house, they will begin to think about the need for sturdy parts like walls and beams to support a roof, doors, and windows.

▶ **Cause and effect:** Cause and effect are about understanding the relationship between what we do (cause) and how it impacts a result or outcome (effect). When children are involved in the hands-on activity of building a house for the three pigs, they observe what happens when they construct a particular structure that then weathers (or does not fare so well) the wolf's huffing and puffing. This helps children develop a basic understanding of how actions and circumstances determine outcomes.

▶ **Shapes and measurement:** In engineering design, shapes affect how structures look and their stability. For instance, when children use round handfuls of Play-Doh for a tower, it can wobble. But using square or rectangular pieces, like bricks, it makes a structure steadier. Measurement ensures that things fit together and work right. For example, children can use rulers or hands to measure an index card to be just the right size and shape for the roof of the house they build for the three pigs.

The activity also engages children in the engineering design process consisting of the following iterative but nonlinear steps:

▶ **Identifying:** Developing the ability to describe and define a problem by asking questions, deciding what needs to be done, and developing a sense of the project's overall goal.

▶ **Imagining:** The ability to visualize possibilities, put them into words, and discuss them with others to explore next steps.

▶ **Planning:** The ability to think through options, choose a possible solution considering the materials and goal, and move forward to next steps.

▶ **Creating:** The ability to build a prototype based on the plan with creativity, imagination, flexibility, and persistence.

▶ **Improving:** The ability to test the prototype, evaluate what is working, improve the design as needed, and learn from failures.

▶ **Communicating:** Being willing and open to using different media to communicate thinking, design possibilities, to make plans and check progress, and to talk through results with the goals of using feedback to consider new possibilities.

Conducting the Assessment

Materials

▶ **Children's book:** There are many versions of *The Three Little Pigs*, and we recommend using a simple one and one written in the child's home language.

▶ **House-building materials:** Play-Doh or clay, coffee stir sticks or craft sticks, masking tape, strong index cards, string, scissors, and trays to hold children's constructions.

▶ **Recording tools:** paper and pencils.

Procedures

▶ **Grouping.** Conduct the activity in small groups of no more than four children at a time. The teacher or provider works with one small group at a time for 30–40 minutes to ensure sufficient attention and documentation of children's questions, design thinking, behavior, and outcome of the work session.

▶ **Duration.** This project can span from a few days to weeks, depending on the available time for children to engage in the various steps. To ensure the project's success, it is important for the teacher or provider to allow sufficient time for small groups to work on their designs and facilitate group discussions throughout the process.

▶ **Flexible steps.** The steps outlined below serve as a general guide, but the teacher or provider can adapt and "chunk" them into smaller steps based on the children's progress and chosen paths. It's important to note that different groups may proceed at different paces. The teacher and provider's role is to closely monitor and guide the group process, identifying areas where children are making progress and areas where they may be encountering challenges or obstacles.

Step 1: Read and discuss the story with the whole group.
Before starting the project, the teacher or provider reads a simple version of the story of *The Three Little Pigs* to the entire class. For three- and young four-year-olds, the provider or teacher may want to tell the story in simple words while using the book illustrations as a guide to a picture walk of the book and story. Read the story two or three times over the period of a week. After each reading, we recommend that the teacher or provider guide the class in acting out the story. This allows the children to see the meaning of the story visually portrayed and enacted up close.

After acting out the story, the teacher or provider engages the children in an open-ended discussion for five to ten minutes by posing one or two thought-provoking questions that explore different aspects of the story. The goal in these discussions is to model for children what it is like to think out loud together about a problem, to experience listening and offering ideas to one another in a way that benefits everyone. In these discussions, there are no right answers, only ideas, possibilities to consider, and more details to wonder about.

When planning discussion questions for this initial story activity, and later when discussing the children's own attempt to build a strong house, it is helpful to think of different kinds of questions to pose to them. There are several frameworks for asking questions that teachers and providers can utilize. We recommend the following categories of questions with suggestions as a starting point:

▶ **Factual questions:** questions that invite children to recall or summarize facts included in the story. For example, "Tell us about the second pig's house. What do we know about that house?" "Tell us about the third pig's house. What do we know about that house?"

▶ **Exploratory questions:** questions that invite children to think more deeply about information in the story. For example, how are the 2nd and 3rd pigs' houses the same? And how are they different? Why did the 2nd pig's house get blown over? What happened to it? Why do you think the sticks didn't hold up to the huffing and puffing? What made the third pig's house strong?

) **Making connections:** As discussions grow, children can be invited to bring information from several sources to think through the problem even more deeply. Such questions might include: When the mother sees the pigs again, what might the pigs tell her? How might the mother pig respond? Had she warned them about the wolf? Did she prepare the pigs for building strong houses?

These questions serve as entry points for open-ended discussions, encouraging children to consider multiple perspectives and interpretations of the story. It is recommended to select one version of the story for repeated readings and focus discussions for around five minutes after each reading session. The purpose of this "studying one story in depth" approach is to ensure that the children become familiar with the story and have opportunities to contemplate the pigs' choices and decisions. The discussions of the story model the kinds of discussions the teacher or provider will support when the children are building their own versions of strong houses.

Step 2: Introduce the project to the whole group. Young children are usually eager to participate in the building process. However, the initial introduction to the activity is key to the success of the construction project because it orients the children to the purpose of the task and important details.

a. **Narrative context and goal:** Gather the children in a large group and introduce the activity with a narrative that connects to the reading and discussions of the storybook. For example, a provider or teacher could say, "Children, we have read and discussed the story of the three pigs several times. Now, we are doing a special project. Each of you will pretend to be a pig and construct a house – a strong one that the big bad wolf cannot blow down. You will first build the house on your own and later you can build one with your friends." Introducing the project in this way engages and motivates the children while helping them understand the problem and goal of the project.

b. **Decision regarding the wolf's huffing and puffing:** An important step is to decide how to simulate the wolf's huffing and puffing to test the strength of the houses. Present three possibilities to the group: having four children from each group blow together, or use a handheld fan, or utilize a portable mini fan. Draw the options on chart paper and discuss the advantages, disadvantages, and practicalities of each choice. Allow the children to vote for their preferred option, reaching a final decision collectively. There needs to be agreement on one option used to test the houses from all groups.

c. **Knowledge of materials:** Explain to children that they will work in small groups of four. Unlike the pigs in the story, each group will receive the same set of materials to build their houses. These materials include clay or Play-Doh, craft sticks or coffee stirrers, scissors, string, index cards, and masking tape. Additionally, each child will have a tray as a base for building the house, and, finally, a piece of paper to draw their house after the construction.

d. **Design requirements:** Remind the children of the project's goal – to construct a strong house for the pigs that can withstand the wolf's blowing. Ask the children what additional features the house should have besides strength, such as a door and roof. Reach a consensus on two required structures for the house. By discussing design requirements, the children adopt the perspective of the clients, the pigs. Encourage them to consider the pigs' needs and preferences for their house, ensuring that the requirements are developmentally appropriate for preschool and kindergarten children – achievable without being overly challenging.

e. **Embracing challenges:** Conclude the discussion by addressing the potential challenge of the house not working as expected initially. Acknowledge the potential emotions that may arise, such as disappointment, frustration, or impatience. Ask the children, "What can we do when we feel upset because our ideas don't work right away?" Remind them that most ideas don't succeed immediately and that it's important to identify problems and find ways to improve. This is what the three pigs had to do. This discussion is essential in preparing the children for the process and helping them navigate potential setbacks and disagreements proactively.

Step 3: Building houses with small groups. When working with each small group, the teacher should guide the children through the following steps:

a. **Explore materials and their properties:** Invite the children to look at, explore, and name the properties of each material. Encourage them to consider questions like, "How does it feel?" "What can it do?" and "How can we use these materials to build a house?" Understanding the properties of different materials is an essential first step in using them properly for construction.

b. **Discuss design possibilities:** Ask children to pause to think about how to make a strong house and how to make the roof and door. Pose questions such as: What shapes will make your house strong? How can you use these materials together to build a strong house? How will you make the roof?

c. **Build a house:** As each child builds, prompt the child to observe how the different materials work together. Provide assistance as necessary while intervening as little as possible, thereby maximizing the children's opportunities to think through difficulties. Discuss the type and shape of materials that provide stability, as well as the kind of door and roof that will not collapse.

d. **Test the house:** Work with the children to test the strength and endurance of their house. Ask them to share their hypotheses regarding how well the house will hold up against the "huffing and puffing" from, for example, the handheld fan acting as the wolf. Perform the huffing and puffing test and ask the children to closely observe any areas of the house's construction that may require strengthening. Encourage discussion about their observations and potential changes. Remain neutral regarding the children's decisions and focus solely on guiding and tracking their thinking through their words. Let the children be responsible for designing, thinking, improving, or choosing not to make any changes. Summarize the huffing and puffing test results for the children and invite them to carry out the necessary actions to enhance the structure of their house.

e. **Make learning visible:** Ask each child to draw their house on paper. Write down the child's response to some of the following questions: "What do you like best about your house?" "What makes it special?" "What made your house strong? The shape of the structure? The type of materials?"

Classroom Snapshot: Ms. Imani's and Her Preschool Children

After several readings and discussions of *The Three Little Pigs* story, Ms. Imani invited a group of four children – Ethan, Noah, Lily, and Mia – to join her in building houses for the three little pigs. The children eagerly gathered around the table during center time to participate in the activity.

Ms. Imani placed four trays on the table, and each tray included a can of Play-Doh, a pack of wooden coffee stir sticks, masking tape, several index cards, and a pair of scissors. Ms. Imani began the activity by asking, "Can someone remind us of what we are doing with these materials?" Lily, brimming with enthusiasm, exclaimed, "We're going to build houses!" Ms. Imani acknowledged Lily's response and added, "Yes, that's exactly what we'll do today. Let's first look at these materials and think about how you might use them to build a *strong* house."

As the children started to select the materials they needed to build their house, Ms. Imani watched attentively. Lily started her work by putting four coffee stir sticks into four small chunks of Play-Doh about one inch around each, making a square. She wanted to make a wall by stacking the sticks, but they kept falling. She looked at Ms. Imani for help. Ms. Imani asked if there were other things on the table to use. Lily made four more Play-Doh balls and connected them to the ends of the sticks. With Ms. Imani's help, she made a cube by connecting all the balls with more sticks. Then, Ms. Imani reminded her she needed a roof and a door on her house. Lily cut an index card and put a piece on top of her structure and then placed a piece in front of the cube.

Ethan built a tall tower by stacking Play-Doh pieces on top of each other with a coffee stir stick in the middle. Excitedly, he called out to Lily, "Look at my tower! I'm making more!" He made two more towers that looked the same. But when he tried to use tape to connect them, he struggled and became disappointed. Sensing his frustration, Ms. Imani asked if he needed help, and Ethan eagerly accepted. Ms. Imani held all three towers while Ethan taped them together a few times. It ended up looking like a tepee.

Meanwhile, Noah taped several sticks together and made a long and thick rod as if it were a sword, proudly announcing, "I'll protect the pigs from the big bad wolf!" He played with the materials for a few minutes but didn't attempt to build a house.

Mia approached her task methodically, declaring, "Hmm... I'm making a strong house. I'll use cards for walls." She laid four index cards on the table but struggled to connect them with tape while holding them vertically. With Ms. Imani's assistance, she built four walls using index cards and placed several coffee stir sticks on the top. Happily, she exclaimed, "My house!"

With excitement, the four children eagerly watched as Ms. Imani switched on a small fan to see how strong their houses were. First up was Lily's cube-shaped house, made with 8 pieces of Play-Doh and 12 sticks. It held up quite well, but when the fan blew, the roof made of index cards got blown away with the "wolf's puff." Lily sighed, saying, "Oh, no."

Ethan eagerly requested, "Test mine, my turn!" His tepee structure withstood the blowing wind, and he joyfully raised his hands in celebration.

Lily asked Noah where his house was, but he shrugged and replied, "I didn't make one." He seemed unconcerned about not having built a house. He replied, "I made a sword to protect them."

At last, Mia's house made of index cards got blown off the table, and the roof, which was made of coffee stir sticks, couldn't stay together when the wind from the fan hit the house. She felt upset and said, "That's not fair!" Ms. Imani comforted Mia saying, "Don't worry. Look, all your walls are still here. You did build a house! What do you think you can do to make it stronger?"

Ms. Imani guided the children in discussing what worked and what did not hold up well. She reminded the four children that the class would talk through the many different challenges everyone is having as well as what worked. In the weeks to follow, their group will work together to build a stronger house. In the meantime, they needed to save their work on their trays in the display area.

At this point, Ms. Imani gave each child a piece of paper and asked them to draw the house they had just built. Lily's drawing showed a square-shaped building with a pointy roof, along with a rectangular door, a chimney, and some fluffy clouds in the sky. Her drawing looked quite different from her actual structure.

Ethan drew a triangle and added three vertical lines inside to show his tepee house.

Noah's drawing had three round pigs, each with ears and tails. He proudly pointed to them and said, "Here are the pigs, and I scared away the big bad wolf!" When asked where the house was, Noah pointed to his head, saying, "It's right here."

Mia quickly sketched a square shape and said, "This is my house." Then she put a big dot on each corner, pointing them out to Ms. Imani and explaining, "I put Play-Doh here to make my house stronger."

Ms. Imani reviewed the children's performance on building and drawing their house and assessed their working approaches using rubrics referencing the cross-cutting STEM concepts and skills in this activity. Noah's performance was marked as Level 0, as he primarily engaged in dramatic play and was not concerned with a house. This Level 0 does not imply that Noah could not build a house. Rather, he was invested in his imaginary plots at the moment and showed little interest in the construction project. For productive and descriptive working approaches, Noah received mixed scores across different levels, indicating varied approaches to learning. In particular, he had five for both chattiness and playfulness for his descriptive working approaches, a sign of his lively social characteristics.

Lily's performance was evaluated as Level 4 because she built a house with a roof that withstood the wolf's huff and puff. She also understood how the materials like coffee stir sticks and Play-Doh work. Her productive and descriptive working approaches showed consistent scores at Level 3.

Mia also received a score of 4 for her house building. Like Lily, her house stayed strong against the wolf. Even though the wind blew her index card house off the table, the structure endured. Further, she showed an interest in improvement when she drew a picture of her house. Mia's scores for productive and descriptive working approaches matched those of Lily.

Finally, Ethan's task performance was rated as Level 5. His tepee showcased a keen awareness of shapes and materials, resulting in the strongest house among the group. For both productive and descriptive working approaches, Ethan received scores of 4 across the board.

Ms. Imani was acutely aware of the limitations of the performance rubric, as it couldn't fully capture the complexity of each child's behavior. In reality, most children exhibited behaviors that spanned multiple levels. Ms. Imani focused on the central points of the rubric when scoring the children's performance. She recognized that the rubric provided an approximate indicator of the essential STEM concepts and skills the children were developing at that moment in time. Using these rough indicators, she knew she was in a good position to plan future activities using the initial assessment data gathered.

Bridging Assessment to Teaching

In a high-quality preschool and childcare setting, children often enthusiastically engage in a variety of playful activities that promote STEM learning. They stack blocks to explore heights, play with shadows and light, and build houses for classroom pets. Integrating these STEM experiences into daily classroom activities provides young learners with opportunities to develop critical thinking, executive functioning, and problem-solving skills, setting the stage for future learning and development across content areas.

After completing the initial Strong House for the Three Pigs activity with all the children, Ms. Imani employed two strategies to bridge the assessment to teaching and learning: First, Ms. Imani organized museum walks to encourage careful observation, communication, and reflection among the children about the first round of houses they built. During the museum walk, the children observed each other's structures, comparing houses for what worked to make them strong. They engaged in discussions about the properties of materials, the relationship between shapes and the strength of structures, and how they held up when there was huffing and puffing. Ms. Imani guided the museum walks by prompting each child to identify specific details they liked about another child's house and pose questions to each builder for further exploration. These structured discussions allowed children to offer feedback, share ideas, and consider different perspectives, enhancing their understanding of house construction.

Second, Ms. Imani created a construction center with various materials and posted pictures of different types of shelters, such as igloos, tepees, huts, and tents, as well as houses from their neighborhood. The materials available in the construction center included Play-Doh, glue sticks, scissors, string, blocks, and recyclable items like cardboard tubes and small containers. These resources encouraged children to explore diverse materials and possibilities for constructing different types of houses.

By utilizing museum walks and providing a rich construction center, Ms. Imani fostered continued exploration, creativity, and critical thinking among the children. For example, she invited each small group back to collaborate on creating a more robust house together this time. She reminded the children of the story of the three pigs, emphasizing the benefits of the pigs working together on the house-building task. For instance, Ethan, Noah, Lily, and Mia were grouped together again, and they began by examining each individual house design, followed by a discussion on how to combine the strengths of these different designs to construct a more robust group project – a stronger house. This collaborative project took place during center time, allowing Ms. Imani to circulate and provide assistance as needed during the discussions and group work. In so doing, she successfully extended the assessment results to inform her curriculum and instruction, facilitating meaningful and engaging learning experiences. Throughout the year, Ms. Imani used the following set of principles to guide her STEM teaching experiences.

Making meaningful STEM connections. STEM activities are most effective when they provide children with opportunities to engage in meaningful learning experiences that connect to their personal and cultural backgrounds, play activities, as well as other areas of the curriculum. For example, children are often fascinated by the idea of growing bigger or taller. Teachers can capitalize on this interest by incorporating resources and activities that explore the concepts of growth and measurement. Storybooks can be valuable tools. Ms. Imani loves the book "*The Knee-High Man*," a traditional Black folktale found in "The Knee-High Man and Other Tales" by Julius Lester, which tells the story of a man who desires to be taller but eventually learns to accept himself as he is. By incorporating such stories into the STEM curriculum, Ms. Imani helps children make connections between their personal experiences of growth and important mathematics and science concepts. This approach not only enhances children's understanding of STEM concepts but also fosters a sense of belonging and cultural relevance in their learning experiences.

Promoting integrated STEM learning. Meaningful STEM connections are rooted in the integration of different disciplines, and this requires intentional planning and thoughtful implementation. For Ms. Imani, one effective approach to meaningful integration is to foreground one specific discipline while allowing others to serve as the background. In the context of the Strong House for Three Pigs activity, Ms. Imani chose to foreground the engineering design process as the primary focus. This involved engaging children in identifying and solving problems using various materials to build a strong house. Meanwhile, mathematics and science could be integrated into the background as children discuss the size and shape of the house. In doing so, Ms. Imani engages the children in a STEM activity while bringing multiple areas of learning together in an authentic way.

Ensuring visible STEM learning and thinking. Ms. Imani knows that STEM learning is enhanced when children's ideas and thought processes are made visible through documentation and communication.

Throughout the STEM activities, she tries to encourage children to express their thinking through various means, such as talking, writing, drawing, or graphing. She documents children's ideas in ways that are comfortable and meaningful for them. For Ms. Imani, it is important to expose her children to working across multiple symbol systems to become proficient in using a variety of tools to express their thinking.

Ms. Imani always takes time to document the learning process, as it can serve as a reference and catalyst for reflection and growth. By documenting their work, Ms. Imani and her children can evaluate and build upon previous ideas, fostering a deeper understanding of STEM concepts. For Ms. Imani, engaging in group or partner learning experiences is a way to deepen skills needed for active participation in a democratic society. These skills include sharing viewpoints, listening to others, considering multiple perspectives, making connections, adapting ideas, and resolving conflicts.

Activating STEM thinking through language use. Over the years, Ms. Imani learned that in STEM learning for young children, hands-on experiences are important, but it is crucial to recognize that understanding does not solely come from the physical manipulation of materials. Language plays a significant role in activating children's thinking and fostering their conceptual understanding. Young children learn not only by doing but also by thinking and talking about what they are doing.

Ms. Imani employs two strategies to activate STEM thinking with language. One is to introduce new scientific vocabulary during the STEM learning experience, words such as "design," "force," and "sturdy." The other is to engage in conversations with children at each step of the activity by asking open-ended questions to encourage children to share their thinking. For example, ask children: "How could the three pigs have known which materials to choose for building their house, or even if they could use all three materials (straw, sticks, and bricks), what would they use for the house?" These conversations help children articulate their ideas, clarify misconceptions, and deepen their thinking. Becoming comfortable with asking questions, wondering about possibilities, has become the hallmark of Ms. Imani's teaching.

Activity Recording Sheets

Pretend Play Recording Sheet

Child's Name_____ Date_____ Minutes in Play_____ Performance Score_____

What did the child do if not engaged in pretend play:

Notes about the child's play:

Objects transformed into something else?

Gestures/movement imitating another character?

Words: What words or conversations does the child have?

Others: Interaction with others? How many other children?

Joint collaboration on an evolving narrative?

Talk during the play episode?

- To create a character
- Talking as the character
- To create scene
- To describe/narrate what's happening
- To direct the actions of others
- To negotiate conflict

Dictating a Story Recording Sheet

Child's Name_____   Date_____   Performance Score_____

Note any observations of child during the activity and record (or staple) child's dictated story here.

Story source

☐ Original story
☐ Shows connections to another child's story or a story book read in class
☐ Retelling of a familiar story

Child begins story easily

☐ no
☐ with prompting
☐ yes

Child can bring story to conclusion

☐ no
☐ with prompting
☐ yes

Acting Out a Story Recording Sheet

Child's Name_____   Date_____   Performance Score_____

Participation

☐ by presence, no speaking

☐ is present, pays attention, follows action

☐ watches others and participates

☐ gestures or speaks with prompting

☐ gestures or speech appears self-initiated

☐ follows group, generally imitates

Body Movement

☐ body appears limp

☐ uses body dynamically to express
   action/feeling of character

Vocal/Facial Expression

☐ speech is monotone, facial expression flat

☐ speech and facial expression are varied

☐ expression used does not correspond to
   situation/character

☐ expression used is accurate, corresponds
   to character/situation

Social Awareness

☐ does not contribute to organization of
   group presentation

☐ contributes to organizing the scenario

☐ cues other children to parts/actions

Use this section to describe what the child does and make notes about the child's experience acting out a story.

Counting Collections Recording Sheet

Child's Name_____ Date_____ Bag ID _____ Performance Score_____

How many items are in the bag?_____

Show how you counted.

Self-Portrait Recording Sheet

Child's Name_____   Date_____   Performance Score_____

Use this page to record notes about what the child says or does while completing a self-portrait. Keep this along with the self-portrait (or copy of it).

Strong House for the Three Pigs Recording Sheet

Child's Name_____   Date_____   Performance Score_____

Record the child's verbal and nonverbal behavior during the house construction process.

Ask the child to look at the house he/she built and draw a picture of it on this page, or attach the child's picture here.

Performance Rubrics

Pretend Play Performance Rubric

LEVEL	NAME	PERFORMANCE INDICATORS
0	No Pretend Play	• No evidence that child is in a make believe/pretend play episode.
1	Playing Alone: Being Someone Else or Objects Become Something Else	• Child is playing alone. • Child announces that he/she is a particular character or declares an object is something other than what it is (e.g., a pencil is a shovel for digging a hole). • Child may add a few gestures to portray the character he/she is pretending to be or to the object he/she pretends to have. • Child manipulates objects (e.g., blocks, beads, clay) and names them or otherwise indicates that the object is something else, a pretend something. • Child may play with words, rhythm, or rhyme of several words, for example, "Wishy washy, dishy dashy, swishy swashy!" • Play might last a short time or carry on for a good long while.
2	Becoming Someone Else With Another Child	• Child announces that he/she is a particular character or declares an object is something other than what it is (e.g., a block is a baby's pillow). • Children are largely in parallel play – 2 scenes unfolding alongside each other. Although playing alongside another, little or no evidence of creating a shared narrative script. • The other child names who and what he/she is doing. The pretend play with another is brief, lasting no more than a minute or two, while the play of each child may continue as in Level 1. • Content of pretend play may shift frequently without elaboration. • Child may add some gestures to the role she or he is enacting. • Children may include a few objects to represent something in the pretend episode (large buttons may become money to pay the grocer, food to feed the baby, or gold that bad guys steal).
3	First Extended Pretend Scenarios With Others	• Child engages in pretend play situation in a role with one or more children. • The use of objects and/or gestures signal the pretend world where the play is taking place (e.g., two girls pretending to be sisters taking care of their sick babies

(Continued)

LEVEL	NAME	PERFORMANCE INDICATORS
		• The verbal exchanges reflect the children's efforts to establish characters and describe the pretend play scene. • The shared pretend play episode with another child is relatively short, perhaps lasting 2–5 minutes.
4	Sustaining Pretend Play Alongside Another	• Child participates in developing a play episode with at least one other child where they begin to coordinate characters and their actions at least some of the time. • Play episode lasts 5+ minutes minimum. • There is verbal interaction among the actors describing what is happening and directing the unfolding story.
5	Developing Interactive Play Skills	• Child participates in setting up and carrying on pretend play situation with at least one other child. • The play episode lasts for 10–15 minutes. • Verbal interaction is moderate both in deciding roles and plot, and in carrying out the story line. • Gestures, movement, and talk are in sync with the pretend setting and its unfolding story line. • Child readily adapts and improvises his or her pretending to new twists and turns in the story line. • Child asserts her or his wishes and when there is no compromise, gets help from a teacher.
6	Interactive Pretend Play	• Child is present and participating in sustained and elaborate pretend play with at least two other children. • Child contributes verbally to elaboration of the pretend play scenario. • Every object, gesture/movement, sound, and utterance reflect the pretend play world. • Play episode lasts for more than 20 minutes. • The child can resolve moments of tension in the play to keep the scene moving; child can help repair disagreements, seeks compromises.

Dictating a Story Performance Rubric

LEVEL	NAME	PERFORMANCE INDICATORS
0	No Participation	• Child declines to participate in activity.
1	First Stories	• Child tells a one-word story such as "Mommy." Or "Running." • Child says one or more words, but without connections among the words. Story can sound like a list of items or events (e.g., "A flower, a pencil, a bunny." • Child may scribble on paper and give one-word label or name to each object. • Story is one sentence (e.g., "A mermaid swims in the water.")
2	Sequence of Events	• Story elements share a common core because of some visible similarity (for example, a certain action repeated over and over or an "events of the day" story). • Story is a collection of ideas/objects/associations linked by some concrete similarity (e.g., "I build a strong house. The wolf cannot blow it. The Pig says, 'I went in my house.'") • There is no single idea or character or problem at the center of the story. • Story might contain little detail or be a string of associations.
3	Primitive Narratives	• There is a core idea or character at the center of the story. • Relations among characters and actions are not fully developed. • The links among the characters and actions are based on practical experience in the here-and-now. The links are concrete rather than conceptual. • Story events lead from one to another, but links may shift (settings may blur, characters may come and go).

(Continued)

LEVEL	NAME	PERFORMANCE INDICATORS
4	Unfocused Chain	• Child's story line is tenuous and often gives way to another topic. • Story events lead from one to another, but links may shift over the course of the story. • Links among story events are often based in the here-and-now and are concrete.
5	Focused Chain – Problems and Plots Emerge	• Story is well developed in terms of events and actions of characters. • The story plot proceeds with a central idea or conflict that is concrete rather than conceptual (e.g., a baby is sick and needs to go to the doctor, a princess has to find her lost sister, or good guys have to stop pirates from kidnapping the captain). • Stories can be a "continuous adventures of ___" type narrative (e.g., "My dog went to the store with me, she watched TV, she went to the park, and she barked at the squirrels.")
6	Elaborate Narrative	• Child's story unfolds with a set of events and characters around a central idea or problem with consistent forward movement toward problem resolution at a conceptual level (e.g., "A lonely fox has no friends and finds a lost rabbit. Will the fox try to eat it or find a way to make friends?"). • Story has a climax where there is change in a character or circumstances as a result of events or characters' actions (e.g., "The lion was sorry he scared the fox, and they became friends. The lion built a hideout right by the fox's hole in the ground by the tree.") • Story includes some description of characters' motivations and indicators of change.

Source: Adapted from Applebee (1978).

Acting Out a Story Performance Rubric

LEVEL	NAME	PERFORMANCE INDICATORS
0	No Participation	• Child declines to participate in activity.
1	Participation by Presence, Nonverbal	• Child agrees/volunteers to participate in story dramatization and is physically present but the child's part as a character is not actually a part of the flow of the story. • Child offers no gestures or actions. • Child does not speak but appears attentive to what is going on; lets narrator convey the child's story part.
2	Participates Verbally With Prompting	• Child is attentive and focused. • Child makes a few gestures with prompting. • Child repeats the lines of her/his character timidly when prompted to do so. • Child's movement, facial expressions, and intonation may not totally correspond to character or situation. • Child's timing of playing out a character's part is not quite in sync with the storyline (e.g., a child playing Batman driving in the Batmobile continues driving around even though the story calls for Batman to capture the bad guys).
3	Participation in a Flow	• Child follows the group rhythm, imitating other children to portray character, part, or lines. • Child watches other children as a reminder of the child's own lines or part or as a way to gauge own actions. • Child may or may not need prompts. • Child speaks lines of character willingly.
4	Beginner Acting Without Prompting	• Child recognizes the part she or he is playing and acts out lines and actions with minimal if any prompting. • Child's speech tends to be in conversational voice. • Child's facial expressions, gestures and movements are limited.

(Continued)

LEVEL	NAME	PERFORMANCE INDICATORS
5	Intermediate Acting	• Child uses movement elements (e.g., timing, spacing, and/or body shape) and varied facial expressions during the dramatization. • Child may use lively character voice and highly expressive intonation. Sound effects may be included.
6	Well-Developed Acting	• Child effectively uses a wide range of movement elements, facial expressions, and lively character voice. • Child cues other children to their parts/actions. • Child contributes to organizing the scenario and has an awareness of the actions of other characters.

Counting Collections Performance Rubric

LEVEL	NAME	PERFORMANCE INDICATORS
0	No Counting	• Child declines to participate in the activity. • Child plays with the materials but does no counting.
1	Knows Some Number Names	• Child names some number words with incorrect order. • Child represents how many counted and how counting was done incorrectly.
2	Uses Correct Counting Word Sequence	• Child uses correct counting word sequence. • Child has no strategy for keeping track of the objects in the collection. • Child draws how many counted and how counting was done incorrectly.
3	Uses 1-1 Correspondence Strategy to Count	• Child uses the correct counting word sequence up to 10. • Child uses 1–1 correspondence strategy to count. • Child answers the "how many" question with the last number counted incorrectly. • Child draws how many counted and how counting was done incorrectly.
4	Counts With Understanding of Cardinality	• Child counts objects accurately up to 10. • Answers the "how many objects" question correctly. • Child represents how many counted and how counting was done correctly. • Child can write numerals to represent the last number counted.

5	Counts With Cardinality and Uses 1–2 Strategies	• Child achieves Level 4 above and one or two of the following:
		  • counts beyond 20 correctly
		  • uses "counting on" to find out how many objects
		  • conceptually subitizes numbers to assist with counting
		  • counts by groups or in units such as by twos (2, 4, 6, 8. . .) or by fives (5, 10, 15. . .)
		  • knows a number combination (e.g., "3 and 7 is 10. I just know it.")
		  • uses organizational tool to assist the counting (lining up or grouping objects to be counted)

(Continued)

LEVEL	NAME	PERFORMANCE INDICATORS
6	Counts With Cardinality and Has Several Strategies for Counting	• Child achieves Level 4 above and three or four of the following: • counts beyond 30 correctly • uses "counting on" to find out how many objects • conceptually subitizes numbers to assist with counting • uses skip counting by 2s, 5s, or 10s • counts in units • knows a number combination • uses organizational tool to assist the counting

Self-Portrait Performance Rubric

LEVEL	NAME	PERFORMANCE INDICATORS
0	No Participation	• Child declines to participate in the activity.
1	Scribbles and Drawing Marks	• Child watches others or makes use of paper and pencil for some other purpose. • Child makes marks on the page, but with no recognizable representation or naming of a person.
2	First Representation of a Person: Stick Figure	• Child draws rudimentary human figure: head with eyes, circle atop two sticks, tadpole-like form. • Child might indicate marks representing others in a setting (e.g., pointing to a circle saying, "This is my bed.")
3	Simple Human Figures	• Child draws rudimentary human figure: head with eyes, circle atop two sticks, tadpole-like form. • People depicted are engaged in an activity, or in the company of other people. • There is some indication or mention of a setting.

4	Human Figures in a Recognizable Setting	• Child draws self and other figures with one or two of the following:
		  • Separate parts for head and body
		  • Facial features (eyes, nose, mouth)
		  • Hands and/or feet
		  • Hair and/or clothing
		• Setting is recognizable as a room, playground, or classroom.

5	Detailed Drawing of People With Detailed Setting	• The drawing has considerable detail in people and setting. Child draws human figure with three or more of the following:
		  • Separate parts for head and body
		  • Facial features (at least both mouth and eyes)
		  • Hands and/or feet
		  • Hair and/or clothing
		• People are portrayed alongside other objects that represent the setting: near a TV, a bike, kitchen table.

(Continued)

LEVEL	NAME	PERFORMANCE INDICATORS
6	Detailed Drawing of People in a Recognizable Setting While Using Artistic Elements	• Child uses one or two of the following artistic elements (elements must be present in both the figure and the setting): • Shading (makes objects look 3D or show light source effect on how objects appear) • Perspective (shows that objects are behind others or farther away; tries to show depth) • Line quality (uses thick/thin, hard/soft, straight/wavy, etc., to indicate mood) • Repeated design elements (unifies picture with border; repeats line/texture pattern) • Proportions of figure(s) to setting or objects are realistic.

Strong House for the Three Pigs Performance Rubric

LEVEL	NAME	PERFORMANCE INDICATORS
0	No Participation	• Child declines to participate in the activity or shows no interest in participation. • Child engages in pretend play unrelated to the needs of the three pigs
1	Sensory Exploration of Materials	• Child plays with the materials by touching and feeling them. • Child explores the textures, feel, and features of materials to see what they can do (e.g., squishy, flexible, sturdy) • Child describes what one is doing with the materials (e.g., I'm making balls. I like to play with string). • Child experiments with creating a simple structure without intending to build a house.
2	Building With Materials	• Child builds a simple structure with some stability without a clear intent to build a house (e.g., stacking Play-Doh pieces together with sticks). • Child begins to use the properties of the materials to serve a goal or create a specific product (e.g., roll out Play-Doh into a snake to create a flexible string-like shape). • Child struggles with why materials won't hold together or hold up as the child hoped. • Child asks for help with specific procedural logistics (e.g., holding two sticks while trying to connect them with tape or string).
3	Simple House Structure	• Child attempts to build a house structure. • Child begins to choose materials intentionally (e.g., using tape or string to connect sticks to form walls or choosing Play-Doh as the floor) • Child asks questions and explores how to use materials to achieve a desired result (e.g., Should I use string or tape to tie sticks together?). • Child discusses ways to keep the house from collapsing (e.g., how to make the walls stand up? What makes them sturdy?)

(Continued)

LEVEL	NAME	PERFORMANCE INDICATORS
4	A House Structure With Stable Walls	• Child focuses on building a house that has stable walls. • Child explores different ways to achieve a design goal (e.g., using more sticks to build a big house.). • Child asks questions that reflect a focus on how to get materials to work to achieve goals with the house building (e.g., "Which is better for building the walls – sticks or index cards?").
5	Sturdy House Structure With Roof and Door	• Child focuses building not only a strong house but one with a more stable roof and functional door or windows. • Child considers the features of materials to determine what combination of shapes, length, thickness of various materials, is most suitable to achieve a stable sturdy house with a roof and door. • Child shows patience with problem-solving and analyzes minor to moderate issues regarding what is not working. • Child looks for ways to fix and enhance the design instead of getting thrown off by failures like a collapsing house.
6	Sturdy House With Details and Complex Structures	• Child creates a stable house structure that includes intricate details and features. • Child demonstrates a solid understanding of material properties, using them creatively to achieve the goal of a sturdy house. • Child builds a structure that optimizes shape and material choices (e.g., is conscious of using rectangular Play-Doh pieces for walls and index cards or sticks for the roof) • Child persists through shortcomings and failures while building. • Child describes, discusses, and debates what's not working and ways to improve the house with teachers and peers.

Working Approaches Rubrics

Productive Working Approach Rubric   Child's Name:_____ Task: _____

Circle the number that best describes the child's productive working approach in this activity.

Initial engagement: How does the child initially respond to the activity?				
Hesitant_____**Eager**				
1	2	3	4	5
very hesitant or unwilling to begin activity		becomes involved	eager to begin activity on his or her own	

Focus and attention: How on-task is the child throughout the activity?				
Distractable _____ **Attentive**				
1	2	3	4	5
very easily distracted by other children, events, or materials		attentive some of the time	sustained, absorbed attention to activity	

Goal orientation: To what extent is the child working toward the activity's goal?				
Personal goal _____**Activity goal**				
1	2	3	4	5
works on personal goal rather than activity goal		vacillates between personal and activity goal	works efficiently toward activity goal	

Planfulness: To what extent is the child organized in working toward task completion?				
Haphazard _____ **Organized**				
1	2	3	4	5
random or impulsive; no evidence of organization of materials or approach		organized some of the time	well-organized, methodical in approach or with materials	

Resourcefulness: What does the child do when stuck?				
Helpless _____ **Resourceful**				
1	2	3	4	5
does not ask for help; unable to use help when offered		moves forward a step when help is offered	seeks help and makes good use of it to figure out challenges	

Cooperation: How does the child work with peers to accomplish the task?				
Difficulty working with others_____ **Helpful to others**				
1	2	3	4	5
has difficulty sharing materials or attention, taking turns, supporting the efforts of others		gets along with other children	helps other children with activity, materials, or as a mediator; models ideas for others	

Descriptive Working Approach Rubric Child's Name:_____ Task: _____

Circle the number that best describes the child's descriptive working approach in this activity.

Chattiness: How much does the child talk during the activity?				
Quiet _____ Chatty				
1	2	3	4	5
little conversation and self-talk throughout the activity		talks from time to time	constantly talks	
Pace of work: What is the child's pace of work?				
Slow _____ Fast				
1	2	3	4	5
slow to start and carry out the activity		moderate pace throughout the activity	quick start and quick finish	
Social referencing: How often does the child check with teachers or peers?				
Little interaction _____ Constant checking				
1	2	3	4	5
focuses on own work		attention to others' work and checks with others about the task occasionally	frequently asks teacher or peer about the task	
Playfulness: How animated, lively, or happy is the child during the activity?				
Serious _____ Playful				
1	2	3	4	5
mood/demeanor is serious and cheerless		business-like with activity	cheerful, sense of humor during the activity	

A Child's Learning Profile Summary

APPENDIX
D

A Child's Learning Profile Summary

Child's Name: Age: Gender:		Pretend Play **Cross-Content Learnings**	Dictating a Story **Language and Literacy**	Acting Out a Story **Language and Literacy**	Counting Collections **Math**	Self-Portrait **Visual Arts**	Strong House for the 3 Pigs **STEM**
Date of assessment							
Performance rubric score							
Productive Working Approaches	Initial engagement						
	Focus and attention						
	Planfulness						
	Goal orientation						
	Resourcefulness						
	Cooperation						
Descriptive Working Approaches	Chattiness						
	Pace of work						
	Social referencing						
	Playfulness						

Glossary

Assessment: Assessment is the process of gathering and then interpreting a body of information for decision-making. For classroom teachers, this process consists of listening, observing, and gathering evidence to evaluate children's learning and developmental status in the classroom context.

Authentic assessment: An authentic assessment in early childhood settings relies on a teacher or provider observing and listening to children at work in the classroom for evidence of what they know and can do. Teachers and providers make a point to notice children solving problems, socially interacting, and making various products such as a puzzle, a drawing, and dance moves. The assessment process is embedded and continuous with normal daily routines and occurs within a familiar environment with supportive individuals.

Content of learning: The content of learning refers to the specific knowledge, skills, and concepts that young children acquire through daily activities and experiences. Content – what children are learning – typically encompasses a wide range of areas such as language and literacy, math, sciences, the arts, physical movement, and social and emotional learning skills.

Criterion-referenced rubric: Rubrics are constructed from a careful study of the connection between a child's performance on a task and the developmental trajectory of how knowledge and skills in a content area unfold. Performance according to a criterion-referenced rubric denotes the child's progress in relation to the content knowledge and skills in that domain of study.

Curriculum-embedded assessment: Teachers observe, document, and analyze children's learning while they are engaged in selected classroom activities from different curricular areas. These activity exemplars from a curriculum area serve as a window for gauging children's developmental progress.

Developmental continuum: A developmental continuum describes changes in children's skills and understanding of concepts in an area of development (for example, learning to read) over the years. A developmental continuum characterizes the qualitative and quantitative shifts that mark the growth and changes in a content area.

Executive functioning: Executive functioning refers to a set of mental processes and skills that help individuals manage and control their thoughts, actions, and emotions in order to achieve a goal and solve problems effectively. For young children, this includes their ability to focus and pay attention, remember instructions, and demonstrate self-control. Young children's executive functioning is still developing and continues to mature throughout childhood and adolescence.

Face validity: Face validity establishes how closely an assessment process and measure coincides with and corresponds to the phenomena being assessed. The face validity of *Bridging* rubrics and each of their six levels describes how each performance level reasonably and accurately corresponds to possible and expected developmental behaviors among children in that content area. They are established through consultation with experts, clinical experience, and the review of relevant professional literature.

Formative assessment: Commonly contrasted with a summative assessment designed to evaluate student learning and achievement after a specific instructional period, a formative assessment is an ongoing data collection process, including observation to help teachers monitor student learning progress, adjust instructions, and provide differentiated support.

Instructional routine: Instructional routines refer to a structured and predictable sequence of activities such as participating in a read aloud, story dictation, or number talk. They provide a framework for educators to offer content area learning in an engaging way for children that facilitates their learning. Instructional routines are designed to achieve specific educational objectives, they offer a low entry point and a high potential for growth, ensuring that all participants of all skill levels can engage and aim for elevated levels of accomplishment. As educators and children become familiar with instructional routines, they know what to anticipate as the activity unfolds thus making learning of content engaging and focused.

Key concepts and skills: Key concepts and skills refer to the underlying core knowledge that is central to the content area of learning, consistent with children's thinking, and generative for future learning. The five counting principles in the Counting Collections activity, for example, represent key math concepts and skills in that activity. When educators understand the fundamental concepts in an activity, they become more focused on guiding children's learning and development in various content areas.

Learning profile: A learning profile in *Bridging* assessment is a visual map portraying a child's current level of performance across a range of content areas along with the child's working approaches while engaged in each activity.

Observational assessments: This term is sometimes used interchangeably with authentic or ongoing or formative assessment. It refers to a systematic process of collecting information and involves educators or observers closely and objectively watching and documenting a child's actions, responses, and performance as they engage in various learning activities and social interactions.

Performance-based assessment: Serving as an alternative to paper-pencil, multiple-choice testing, performance-based assessments invite children to create a product or perform a task that demonstrates the student's knowledge, skills, and understandings.

Performance rubric: Performance rubrics are behavioral indicators that describe different levels of performance in a range of curricular activities. Each level of performance marks a developmental step toward mastery of specific concepts and skills.

Process of learning: The process of learning is concerned with the "how" of learning – how children learn in contrast to the content of learning or "what" is being learned. It describes how children perceive, engage, and approach learning tasks. In *Bridging* assessment, it includes a detailed examination of individual children's productive and descriptive learning approaches.

Self-regulation: Self-regulation in early childhood refers to the gradual development of a child's ability to manage their emotions, behaviors, and impulses in a way that allows them to function effectively in various social and learning contexts. It includes skills such as managing one's emotions, impulses, attention, focus, and goal-oriented behavior. It helps children get along with others while maintaining a strong working sense of self.

Working approach: A working approach describes how a child interacts with materials, peers, and adults while responding to the demands of a task in a specific subject area. Working approaches are not a set of stable traits in the child but are malleable and affected by an educator's guidance and coaching. *Bridging* includes productive and descriptive working approaches. Productive working approaches hinder or enhance a child's performance on a task. Descriptive working approaches are just that – descriptions of characteristics or personality differences in how children engage in learning.

Bibliography

Applebee, A. (1978). *The child's concept of story: Ages two to seventeen.* University of Chicago Press.

Bruner, J. (1966). On cognitive growth. In J. Bruner, R. Olver, & P. M. Greenfield (Eds.), *Studies in cognitive growth* (pp. 1–29). Wiley.

Chen, J. Q., Masur, A., & McNamee, G. D. (2011). Young children's approaches to learning: A sociocultural perspective. *Early Child Development and Care, 181*(8), 1137–1152.

Chen, J. Q., & McNamee, G. D. (2006). Strengthening early childhood teacher preparation: Integrating assessment, curriculum development and instructional practice in student teaching. *Journal of Early Childhood Teacher Education, 27,* 109–128.

Chen, J. Q., & McNamee, G. D. (2007). *Bridging: Assessment for teaching and learning in early childhood classrooms, preK–3.* Corwin.

Chen, J. Q., & McNamee, G. D. (2010). Young children's approaches to learning: A sociocultural perspective. *Early Childhood Development and Care,* 1–16. https://doi.org/10.1080/03004430.2010.520160

Chen, J. Q., & McNamee, G. D. (2011). Positive approaches to learning in the context of preschool classroom activities. *Journal of Early Childhood Teacher Education, 39,* 71–78.

Claessens, A., & Engel, M. (2013). How important is where you start? Early mathematics knowledge and later school success. *Teachers College Record, 115*(6). https://doi.org/10.1177/016146811311500603

Cole, M., & Scribner, S. (1974). *Culture and thought: A psychological introduction.* John Wiley.

Common Core State Standards for Mathematics. (2023). https://learning.ccsso.org/common-core-state-standards-initiative

Curenton, S. M., Iruka, I. U., Humphries, M., Jensen, B., Durden, T., Rochester, S. E., & Kinzie, M. B. (2020). Validity for the Assessing Classroom Sociocultural Equity Scale (ACSES) in early childhood classrooms. *Early Education and Development, 31*(2), 284–303.

Darling-Hammond, L., & Baratz-Snowden, J. (Eds.). (2005). *A good teacher in every classroom: Preparing the highly qualified teachers our children deserve.* Jossey-Bass.

Duncan, G. J., Dowsett, C. J., Claessens, A., Magnuson, K., Huston, A. C., Klebanov, P., & Japel, C. (2007). School readiness and later achievement. *Developmental Psychology, 43*(6), 1428–1446.

Franke, M. L., Kazemi, E., & Turrou, A. C. (2018). *Choral counting and counting collections: Transforming the Prek-5 math classroom.* Stenhouse.

Geary, D. C., Hoard, M. K., Nugent, L., & Bailey, D. H. (2013). Adolescents' functional numeracy is predicted by their school entry number system knowledge. *PLoS One, 8*(1), e54651. https://doi.org/10.1371/journal.pone.0054651

Griffin, P., & Cole, M. (1984). Current activity for the future: The zo-ped. In B. Rogoff & J. V. Wertsch (Eds.), *New directions for child development* (No. 23, pp. 45–64). Jossey-Bass.

Leont'ev, A. N. (1978). *Activity, consciousness, and personality.* Prentice Hall.

Leont'ev, A. N. (1981). The problem of activity in psychology. In J. W. Werstch (Ed.), *The concept of activity in Soviet psychology* (pp. 37–71). Sharpe.

McNamee, G. D., Chen, J. Q., Masur, A., McCray, J., & Melendez, L. (2008). Assessing and teaching diverse learners. *Journal of Early Childhood Teacher Education, 23*(2), 275–282.

National Association for the Education of Young Children (NAEYC). (2019). *Advancing* equity in early childhood education. Position Statement. Author.

National Council of Teachers of Mathematics. (2006). *Curriculum focal points for prekindergarten through grade 8 mathematics: A quest for coherence.* NCTM.

Paley, V. G. (1981). *Wally's stories: Conversations in the kindergarten.* Harvard University Press.

Paley, V. G. (1986). *Mollie is three, growing up in school.* University of Chicago Press.

Paley, V. G. (1990). *The boy who would be a helicopter: The uses of storytelling in the classroom.* Harvard University Press.

Paley, V. (2001). *In Mrs. Tully's room: A childcare portrait.* Harvard University Press.

Paley, V. G. (2004). *A child's work: The importance of fantasy play.* University of Chicago Press.

Shulman, L. (1986). Those who understand: Knowledge growth in teaching. *Educational Researcher, 15*(2), 4–14.

Shulman, L. (1987). Knowledge and teaching: Foundations of the new reform. *Harvard Educational Review, 57*(1), 1–22.

Smilansky, S. (1968). *The effects of sociodramatic play on disadvantaged preschool children.* John Wiley and Sons.

Smilansky, S., & Shefatya, L. (1990). *Facilitating play: A medium for promoting cognitive, social-emotional, and academic development in young children.* Psychological and Educational Publications.

Smith, N. R., with Fucigna, C., Kennedy, M., & Lord, L. (1993). *Experience and art: Teaching children to paint.* Teachers College Press.

Storytelling and story acting with Vivian Gussin Paley [Video]. (2002). Ball State University, Indiana Center on Early Childhood Development. http://www.naeyc.org

ten Braak, D., Lenes, R., Purpura, D. J., Schmitt, S. A., & Størksen, I. (2022). Why do early mathematics skills predict later mathematics and reading achievement? The role of executive function. *Journal of Experimental Child Psychology, 214,* 105306. https://doi.org/10.1016/j.jecp.2021.105306

The Early Math Collaborative. (2014). *Big ideas of early mathematics: What teachers of young children need to know.* Pearson.

Tobin, J., Hsuch, Y., & Karasawa, M. (2009). *Preschool in three cultures revisited: Japan, China, and the United States.* University of Chicago Press.

Van de Walle, J., Lovin, L. A., Karp, K. S., & Bay-Williams, J. M. (2021). *Teaching student-centered mathematics: Developmentally appropriate instruction for grades PreK-2* (3rd ed.). Pearson.

Vygotsky, L. S. (1978). *Mind in society.* Harvard University Press.

Index

A Sage Company

CORWIN HAS ONE MISSION: to enhance education through intentional professional learning.

We build long-term relationships with our authors, educators, clients, and associations who partner with us to develop and continuously improve the best evidence-based practices that establish and support lifelong learning.